Advance Praise for *Choose Hope*

"Our survival requires that we turn from war and bloodshed to conciliation and discussion. This inspiring book shows that dialogue is good not only between opponents but is also creatively stimulating among advocates of peace."

—The Dalai Lama

"In a world where the only superpower asserts the right to possess thousands of nuclear weapons indefinitely and has announced plans to build 'new, more usable nuclear weapons,' it is obvious that humankind remains in mortal danger. *Choose Hope* offers the fascinating, deeply held views of two activists who are working hard to lessen nuclear dangers. David Krieger and Daisaku Ikeda identify positive measures to be taken by citizens of the world in order to increase the hope that global annihilation need not be the inexorable outcome of more than fifty-five years of nuclear folly."

—Admiral Eugene Carroll, former deputy director of the Center for Defense Information

"It is impossible to separate threats to the ocean, to the environment, and to life itself from the nuclear industry. *Choose Hope* helps us to recover our sanity and to make the choice between life or nuclear death and suffering, and reminds us that our choice matters, now more than ever."

—Jean-Michel Cousteau, president, Ocean Futures Society

CHOOSE HOPE

CHOOSE HOPE

YOUR ROLE IN WAGING PEACE
IN THE NUCLEAR AGE

David Krieger & Daisaku Ikeda

Translated by Richard L. Gage

MIDDLEWAY
P R E S S

Editor's note: This book was originally published in
Japan in August 2001. For this English-language edition, working closely with the authors, we rearranged,
revised and updated the text of the Japanese edition.
We trust this edited version will best convey the
author's intentions to the English-speaking world.

Originally published as *Kibo no Sentaku*,
by Kawado Shobo Shinsha, Tokyo
© 2001 Daisaku Ikeda and David Krieger

Published by Middleway Press
A division of the SGI-USA
606 Wilshire Blvd., Santa Monica, CA 90401

© 2002 Soka Gakkai and David Krieger
ISBN 0-9674697-6-7

10 9 8 7 6 5 4 3

Cover and interior design by Gopa & Ted2

Library of Congress Cataloging-in-Publication Data
Krieger, David.
 [Kibo no sentaku. English]
 Choose hope : your role in waging peace in the nuclear age /
David Krieger and Daisaku Ikeda ; translated by Richard L. Gage.
  p. cm.
Includes bibliographical references and index.
 ISBN 0-9674697-6-7 (hbk. : alk. paper)
 1. Peace. I. Ikeda, Daisaku. II. Title.
JZ5538 .K7513 2002
 327.1'747—dc21
                        2002008416

Contents

Prefaces to the English Edition

There are days when it is difficult to have hope. The newspapers are filled with stories of wars, terrorism and human suffering. There are times when our hope for humanity is seriously challenged by the actions or inactions of individuals and societies across the globe.

We all have a choice. We can submit to apathy and indifference or we can choose hope. This dialogue is about choosing hope and recognizing that we each have a responsibility to make a difference in the world. In this book, Daisaku Ikeda and I are not saying that choosing hope is a simple, easy solution to life and humanity's serious problems. We are only saying that it is necessary if we are to create a better future. We are asking you to consider being part of the solution to the grave problems that confront humanity.

Foremost among these problems is the ever-present danger of nuclear weapons. These weapons, which really are not weapons at all but instruments of annihilation, place humanity's future in jeopardy. As long as some countries rely on nuclear weapons for security, all countries and all people are threatened.

After the terrorist attacks of September 11, 2001, the dangers of nuclear terrorism loom large. September 11 taught us that even the most powerful nations are not immune from terrorist attacks. All are vulnerable, and the weak and despairing have certain advantages in their battles with the rich and powerful. Had terrorists had nuclear weapons on September 11, the death toll could have been three hundred thousand or three million instead of three thousand.

The citizens of rich nations can no longer feel secure in a world in which large numbers of people live in utter despair. No castle walls can be built high enough or strong enough to protect the rich from those who have given up hope for their future. No military preparations or expenditures will in the end be able to protect the rich from suicidal terrorists, particularly those armed with weapons of mass destruction. The world will either be made more just and decent for all, or it will be secure for none.

The issue of nuclear threat, whether by terrorists or governments, like so many other critical issues, is surrounded by thick layers of ignorance and apathy. To change the world, we must bring forth butterflies of hope from the cocoons of ignorance and apathy that surround them. The best place to begin is with ourselves. We must emerge from our own cocoons as positive agents of change.

In this dialogue, we explore our own lives and views of the world. We share with each other and with you, the reader, our views on achieving a more just and peaceful world. We believe deeply that the world can and must be made more decent for all. This is true not only because it is moral and right, but also because if it is not done, those who are injured, alienated and hateful will wreak havoc, tearing down the castle walls and the castle itself. In our Nuclear Age, the demise of civilization and humanity itself could be the price of failure.

We have reached a point in human history that demands more from each of us. It is not just leaders who make history.

It is all of us. By our decisions each day we help shape the world, for better or for worse. On the path to building a better world, a first step is to choose hope. It is only a first step, but it is a critical one, one that will provide the impetus to move forward. There is much to do and you are needed more than perhaps you can imagine.

David Krieger
President
Nuclear Age Peace Foundation

In the words of the great representative of the American Renaissance Ralph Waldo Emerson, whose works I started reading in my youth, "It is really a thought that has built this portentous war-establishment, and a thought shall also melt it away."[1]

Two global wars and a series of ideological and racial conflicts made the twentieth truly a century of war and violence. We must remember, however, that the same century witnessed the worldwide spread of popular movements aimed at peace and disarmament, such as those sponsored by nongovernmental organizations. Some memorable achievements in this direction are the World Court Project, which raised in the International Court of Justice the issue of the illegality of nuclear arms, and the treaty obtained by the International Campaign to Ban Landmines. As such developments indicate, popular solidarity is breaking through the hard wall of harsh reality and altering conventional thinking about security. In the same direction, we of the Soka Gakkai International have joined forces with David Krieger and the Nuclear Age Peace Foundation he heads in the Abolition 2000 drive to eliminate nuclear weapons.

Such movements stimulate a swelling tide of hope. In this book, Dr. Krieger and I examine various outlooks in a search for a philosophy and a vision that will make *hope* the byword of all humanity in the twenty-first century.

Our range of topics includes the roles of the United Nations and nongovernmental organizations and the mission and responsibilities of science and education. We have attempted to plot a path for a world free of war and nuclear weapons. We agree that a conversion from state security to human security is essential if we are to reform our times lastingly.

In Dr. Krieger's words: "Human security...demands protection of the environment and protection against human-rights abuses. It demands an end to poverty as well as to war and genocide. It demands an end to the threat of nuclear holocaust. It demands a judicial system capable of holding states and individuals accountable for violations of international law and a system of nonviolent conflict-resolution.

"The power of our technologies makes our problems global. No nation by itself can protect its citizens from them. National security now requires common security, just as human security demands global security."

On September 11, 2001, terrorist attacks took many precious lives in the United States and roused sorrow and anger in many parts of the world. We must accept the challenge to convert that sorrow and anger into resoluteness and energy for peace. In this way we can help create a world of security and happiness for everyone.

As Dr. Krieger strongly asserts, the destiny of twenty-first-century humanity depends on ensuring worldwide safety and security. Terrorism can be said to epitomize inhumanity. Converting its negative into the positive of a global society radiant with humanism requires pooling all our wisdom supported by the solidarity of all the peoples of the earth.

Today I am more than ever convinced that though our situation may be difficult, we must not stand idly by. In the twenty-first century, humanity must show how mighty "people power" can be. We must make recognition of that power the hallmark of the age.

Despite spates of bad news and crises typified by the dark clouds of trouble hovering over the Middle East, steady hope-giving progress is being made in many areas. One important development in that direction is the expected establishment, in 2003, of the International Criminal Court, which is a real step toward freeing justice from emotion and ending the violence/hatred chain reaction. In our dialogue, Dr. Krieger and I discuss the need for an organization of this kind, too. UN Secretary-General Kofi Annan has called the court a "new international institution, which can help end the culture of impunity and make the twenty-first century qualitatively different from the twentieth."

On the environmental front, the drive for the adoption of the Earth Charter gains impetus. This year, a decade after the UN Conference on Environment and Development, the World Conference in South Africa will concentrate on both creating international systems of cooperation and setting norms of human behavior.

The British historian Arnold J. Toynbee said that, when we view the future of humanity in millennial units, we see that ultimately history is created by "deeper, slower movements."[2]

In our present situation, choices we must make deep within ourselves will determine whether the twenty-first century follows the violent, bellicose path of the twentieth century or leads humanity to an age of peace and harmonious symbiotic living.

Though it may seem roundabout, actually the one way open to us is person-to-person dialogue generating wave after wave of pacifism. Both Dr. Krieger and I have experienced the horror of war. It will make us extremely happy if our dialogue inspires young people to undertake further dialogue for the sake of peace.

Daisaku Ikeda
President
Soka Gakkai International

 Prefaces to the Japanese Edition

Hope does not just occur. It is a conscious choice, an act of will. One must choose hope in the face of all we know.

When one surveys the world, however, there is so much that is *not* hopeful. There is far too much poverty with all the tragedy that accompanies it. There is far too much violence and there are far too many weapons. Someone examining the budgets of the world's countries might conclude that most countries care more about weapons for their militaries than they do about their people.

In a millennial report, the UN secretary-general found that if the world were a village of a thousand people, then only 150 of the inhabitants would live in an affluent area while 780 would live in poor districts and seventy would be in transition. Of the thousand people, two hundred would dispose of 86 percent of the wealth, and nearly half of the villagers would be living on less than two dollars per day

The secretary-general reported that these problems of poverty and disparity make peace unpredictable. He also reported that the environment is also suffering and the quality of the air and water, essential to life, is deteriorating. "Who among us," the secretary-general asked, "would not wonder how long a village in this state can survive?"

A clear-eyed view of the present circumstances on earth is not cause for celebration. Political leaders at all levels seem more focused on shortsighted gains for themselves than on the welfare of humanity. The world's states continue to operate largely in a competitive mode, while increasing numbers of people throughout the world cry out for new modes of cooperation. The corporations that dominate the world's economy continue to base their success on short-term profits and to treat the earth, air and water as economic externalities at their disposal.

I have not yet mentioned the murderers, the merely greedy, and those who are responsible for racism and ethnic cleansing and for the proliferation, use and creation of weapons.

A good argument could be made for giving up on the human species in hopelessness and despair. Perhaps our species is simply acting out a death wish by its selfish, short-sighted and cruel behavior. And yet, we know at a deep level that we are capable of far better than this.

We are a species gifted in the creation of sublime beauty. We are a species capable of love, friendship, loyalty and acts of great selflessness. We are capable of seeing the bigger picture and embracing the challenge of building a better world. Like our technologies, we are dual-purpose. We are capable of both good and evil, and we struggle forward in this world where good and evil continue to co-exist.

I choose hope. It is a conscious choice, made in the full understanding that the evil around us is enough to envelop and overwhelm us. I choose hope because I feel a deep responsibility to do what I believe I am obligated to do—to pass the world on a better place than when I came into it. It is what gives meaning to life. To fight for a better world is a form of living life to its fullest and richest. I choose hope as a personal and professional responsibility.

To explore the meaning of choosing hope in our far-from-perfect world with Daisaku Ikeda, a scholar of Buddhism and leader of an important Buddhist organization, was a privilege and honor. I found in Mr. Ikeda a man with clear commitments to creating a better world. Daisaku Ikeda is a builder and, in his own way, a revolutionary. He seeks a human revolution built on changing people's hearts one by one. I found Daisaku Ikeda to be a man committed to crossing all boundaries in the pursuit of peace and human decency. And, of course, we share a strong commitment to ridding the world of nuclear weapons.

While traveling through Japan and thinking about my friend and dialogue partner, I was struck by the clarity of his commitment and the strength of his voice. With this in mind, I wrote this short poem.

Voice of a Bell
For Daisaku Ikeda

As we travel on this journey
I hear your voice clearly
like the voice of a bell
ringing out for peace

Your vision is reflected
in bright eyes and smiling faces.
I hear your voice clearly
in the voice of the people—

the earnest, the seeker,
the questioner, the worker,
the pilgrim, the sage.
I hear your voice clearly

like the sharp, solid voice
the pure, open voice
of a bell ringing out
again and again for peace.

Dialogue is a way that probes and explores, a way from which hopefully both participants grow in their own understanding of the world. The world needs more dialogue, but dialogue that is aimed at action.

Words must lead to change — in the case of this dialogue, to creating a better world. Building a better world requires hope. Without hope it is not possible to go forward. To choose hope is already a step in the right direction. It is as easy to choose hope as it is to deny it and push it away. With hope, we can change the world.

Each of us must decide whether or not to choose hope. Our dialogue will have succeeded if it helps you to choose hope and act for a better world.

David Krieger
Santa Barbara, California
August 6, 2001

The great French writer Victor Hugo triumphed over a life of turmoil and oppression. Soka University of America possesses a portrait photograph of him in his later years, which bears a handwritten inscription of which I am extremely fond. In English, it means, "Where there is hope, there is peace." If hope is wanting, we must create it for ourselves. Once we have done so, the great wave of peace can swell and spread freely.

I first met Dr. David Krieger, founder and president of the Nuclear Age Peace Foundation and champion of hope and peace, in September 1997, at the World Peace Youth Music Festival in Yokohama. Representatives from fifty-one nations attended the festival to commemorate the fortieth anniversary of my mentor Josei Toda's Declaration for the Abolition of Nuclear Weapons. Mr. Toda delivered his historic declaration at the Mitsuzawa Yokohama Stadium to a throng of fifty thousand young people on September 8, 1957, when the harsh reality of the East-West Cold War gripped the world. In it he denounced nuclear weapons as an absolute evil fundamentally threatening the dignity and right to live of all humanity. He designated their elimination as the first article in his bequest to the youth. Like the roar of a lion of hope, his words emerged from the power of life, which is far greater than nuclear power. Taking its point of origin from this declaration, the Soka Gakkai International peace movement has used the power of dialogue to demolish barriers of opposition and distrust and to build bridges of amity and reliance worldwide.

In the years since then, I have commemorated September 8 by proposing the normalization of bilateral relations between China and Japan in 1968 and, soon after my talks with Chinese leaders, by visiting the Soviet Union in 1974. When the Cold War was over, I regarded it as an opportunity to reinforce and deepen the pacifist current and resolved to redouble my efforts.

It was in the midst of my efforts in citizen diplomacy that I first had the good fortune to meet Dr. Krieger.

In 1982, when tensions between the Soviet Union and the United States were increasing, Dr. Krieger founded the

Nuclear Age Peace Foundation. He played a central role in the work of Abolition 2000, a network of nongovernmental organizations all over the world working for the elimination of nuclear weapons. In addition, he is a member of the Middle Powers Initiative, a source of various ambitious proposals. Under the slogan "Sowing Seeds of Peace," he devotes great effort to the pacifist education of young people, who are a mainstay of his organization's activities.

As if in response to these efforts, in a short period, the Soka Gakkai's promising young successors accomplished the historic task of collecting thirteen million signatures on the Abolition 2000 petition. Presentation of the petition took place during ceremonies in February 1998 in Hiroshima, a place of immense significance to peace activities. At the time, Dr. Krieger said: "Each signature represents a voice of hope, which, together, amounts to a great chorus of hope capable of influencing the whole world."

A few days later, he and I met again, six months after our previous meeting, this time at the Soka Gakkai Okinawa Training Center, which, once a missile site, has been recreated as a fortress of peace. We discussed a full range of significant issues. For instance, agreeing on the importance of training the youth of the world to create a nuclear-free age and of evoking the spiritual power to accomplish this mission, we concluded that popular solidarity must become the new global superpower. It was at this time that we decided to conduct a dialogue, which, on the spot, we titled *Choose Hope*. The word *hope* embodies our boundless expectations of and confidence in young people.

Our dialogue covers many such different themes as the meaning of the Nuclear Age, the route to the elimination of nuclear arms, empowering peace movements, the role of the United Nations and NGOs, the mission of education, and science and humanity. An active poet, Dr. Krieger joined me in discussing the restoration of the poetic spirit in contemporary civilization.

Behind his intellectual, straightforward words, I sense both highly tempered beliefs and blazing passion. Although in the work of creating a peaceful movement he must have encountered storms of malicious criticism and barriers of misunderstanding, Dr. Krieger and his wife and fellow peace champion, Carolee Krieger, have consistently moved forward boldly and optimistically, never retreating a step. Albert Einstein equated energy and mass in his famous equation $E=mc^2$. In a similar and unforgettable way, in words of great faith, Dr. Krieger equates the human spirit with limitless power. Indeed, human will does contain the source of power to defeat the evil that causes war and to enable us not only to survive but also to reform the world. The fate of humanity in the twenty-first century depends on whether we can devise a peace equation stimulating the boundless manifestation of the power of hope inherent in life.

If this book provides suggestions for ways to build a global society of peace and harmonious coexistence free of nuclear weapons and war, Dr. Krieger and I shall be very happy. At the dawn of the twenty-first century, *Choose Hope* represents a first step. My cherished wish is that, from this step, young people will move forward in a brighter, more vigorous march of glory and triumph.

In conclusion, I would like to extend my heartfelt thanks to Shigeo Wakamori, president of the publishing house Kawade Shobo Shinsha, and to Ichiro Ikumi, director of the editorial department, for their unsparing efforts in the production of this book.

August 6, 2001
Daisaku Ikeda
Dedicated to my mentor

PART ONE

THE POWER OF THE INDIVIDUAL

CHAPTER ONE

Peace,
Imagination and Action

The Twenty-first Can Be a Nuclear Weapons—Free Century

Ikeda: Today, we confront the need to turn human history away from its customary course of war and violence and toward peace and harmonious coexistence. One of the most important aspects of the task is the abolition of nuclear weapons.

The nuclear arsenals in the world today are many thousands of times more powerful than the atomic bombs dropped on Hiroshima and Nagasaki. Nonetheless, political and military interests avert our eyes from this tremendous danger.

Author Jonathan Schell sounded an alarm some time ago in his now-classic bestseller *The Fate of the Earth,* in which he spoke of the "death of death."[1] After a nuclear war, death would cease to exist because life would be no more.

Krieger: It is difficult to imagine a world without life, but nuclear weapons make such a world possible, at least for much of life that includes humans. Without humans, there can be no history. Without humans, there is no possibility to interpret and convey the past to the future. The end of human life would mean the end of human intelligence, creativity and, ironically, the application of technologies.

If other intelligent life exists in the universe, perhaps future space archaeologists coming to earth would discern that our species reached this critical juncture and failed to muster the will to control its own species-threatening technologies. I doubt they could ascertain *why* we failed. But if they visit earth within the first 240,000 years after our annihilation, traces of plutonium 239 in the environment would alert them to *how* we failed.

Ikeda: Of course, this is only an imagined possibility related to the common threat we face. But imagination might be the key to meeting the historical challenge confronting us. If we can imagine a future void of human beings, surely we can act to prevent such a future.

That is why the alarm must continually be sounded to wake the peoples of the earth and their leaders. Unless we stimulate a movement to abolish nuclear weapons, our world may be destroyed. That is why I greatly admire the way you speak out courageously against the threat and folly of nuclear weapons and do all you can to create a world free of them.

Choosing Hope

Krieger: Thank you. I equally admire your long commitment to nuclear-weapons abolition. Among the hopeful evidence of movement toward that end have been initiatives undertaken by the youth of your organization, the Soka Gakkai International.[2]

I believe that leadership for peace requires deliberately choosing to be hopeful. We could just as easily opt for despair, ridicule or anger. But only the hope of changing the world opens new vistas.

The nature of hope is determined by individual values. What we need is not narrow, self-centered hope but hope on an ego-surpassing and far-reaching scale.

Ikeda: Your remarks accord with the Buddhist teaching of emphasizing the greater self in preference to the smaller self. In spite of all hardships and complications, our task is to persevere in the hope that the twenty-first can be a nuclear weapons–free century. To realize that goal, it is vital to start with the realization that we live constantly with the threat.

The British philosopher Bertrand Russell acutely exposed the ethical ruin of our Nuclear Age. Russell, noting that our world has germinated strange concepts and distorted morality regarding security, pointed out the irony of a world in which weapons are precious things securely kept, while children are exposed to the danger of nuclear incineration.

That we take pains to protect weapons while we expose children—the future of the race—to peril is impermissible. To ignore this absurdity will spell defeat for humanity. We must not live to destroy. We have the spiritual power to create peace and happiness.

Nelson Mandela's Struggle

Krieger: That power is within us. All it takes is one person to choose hope, to choose to make a difference, and the world will change.

Ikeda: Pioneers of new epochs have always stood independently for their ideals and faith. For instance, the struggles of a hero like Nelson Mandela brought down the infamous apartheid system in South Africa. While the ten thousand days he spent in prison might have obliterated courage and hope in ordinary people, Mandela never retreated a step. When the outside world learned of his staunch battle, people began supporting him and distancing themselves from the unjust South African regime. Then, as I still vividly remember, hope dawned.

In October 1990, six months after his release, Mandela visited Japan as deputy president of the African National Congress. Even then, at our first meeting, I sensed the indomitable will behind his gentle expression and could see he was compelled not by hatred of white people, as his critics suggested, but by compassionate love for all humanity.

Krieger: Though Mandela, during his years in prison, had every reason to despair, his story is filled with hope. He sought to overthrow a powerful, entrenched, racist regime in a country where whites had dominated blacks for centuries. Throughout his twenty-seven years of imprisonment, he persevered and retained the conviction that human dignity must triumph over racism. And, in the end, he succeeded. His seemingly impossible dream became a reality. After release from prison, he became the first black man to be elected president of South Africa.

Ikeda: His aim was not to replace whites with blacks, as some said, but to build a society where all could live in equality. As he said after his release: "It is an ideal which I hope to live for and to achieve. But if needs be, it is an ideal for which I am prepared to die."[3]

Krieger: Such accomplishments are not possible without strong conviction. The greatest aspect of Nelson Mandela's story was his spirit of forgiveness after assuming power. After his long, hard struggle, he was neither bitter nor vindictive. He demonstrated his true stature as a human being by seeking to uphold human dignity for all, even the oppressors.

Scientists for the Abolition of Nuclear Arms

Krieger: Einstein is another of my heroes. He was certainly one of the greatest scientists of all time. Yet, more important for me, he was a great human being who never lost his humanity and who spoke out clearly about the dangers of the Nuclear Age. Prophetically he said, "The unleashed power of the atom has changed everything save our modes of thinking, and thus we drift towards unparalleled catastrophe."[4] He understood that humankind had entered a new era, one that demands a change in our modes of thought.

Ikeda: Einstein knew that nuclear weapons development affects matters much more fundamental than mere techno-scientific progress. In April 1955, just before his death, he joined with Bertrand Russell and others to issue the Russell-Einstein Manifesto. This probing of how human beings should live in the Nuclear Age might be called their testament to humanity.

Krieger: I consider the Russell-Einstein Manifesto one of the most important statements of the twentieth century. Basically, it says that humankind has a choice about the future: "There lies before us, if we choose, continual progress in happiness, knowledge and wisdom. Shall we, instead, choose death, because we cannot forget our quarrels? We appeal as human beings to human beings: Remember your humanity, and forget the rest. If you can do so, the way lies open to a new Paradise; if you cannot, there lies before you the risk of universal death."

Humanity always has a choice about the future, but to choose the path of peace, justice and human dignity requires leaders of extraordinary commitment and perseverance.

Ikeda: Peace and democracy cannot be achieved in a day. But, according to a hard and fast historical principle, one brave person willing to lay down his or her life for a cause will always find a way out of all difficulties. Mandela's example shows how one person of conviction can initiate progress toward many triumphs. The thirteenth-century Buddhist reformer, Nichiren —whose teachings we in the SGI practice—wrote, "One is the mother of ten thousand."[5] The courage of one person transmits itself to others until there are ten thousand courageous people moving triumphantly forward.

Krieger: Another courageous person whom I greatly respect is Joseph Rotblat, one of the eleven signers of the Russell-Einstein Manifesto. He has long been a leader in the global effort to rid the world of nuclear weapons. In the 1940s, he worked on British and American projects to produce an atomic bomb. He believed that the only reason for creating such weapons was to deter the Germans from using them. Then, when it became clear the Germans would not develop an atomic weapon, he left the Manhattan Project, the American project that was then close to creating the first atomic weapons. He was the only scientist to do so. That in itself is admirable. Even more admirable has been his dedication for more than fifty years to ending the nuclear threat to humankind.

Ikeda: Rotblat has said that war has the power to make foolish animals of human beings, and that even normally prudent and sensible scientists lose the ability to make sound judgments once war starts. On the basis of the Russell-Einstein Manifesto, he and others created the Pugwash Conferences on Science and World Affairs, of which, after serving as chairman for forty years, he is now the honorary chairman. Rotblat's efforts to set people on the correct track again are highly admirable.

Krieger: The Pugwash Conferences have brought together scientists from East and West to discuss common dangers. Wherever Joseph Rotblat speaks, he has a simple message for scientists and the world at large: Remember your humanity. This was the title of the lecture he delivered in 1995, when he and the Pugwash Conferences shared the Nobel Peace Prize.

Ikeda: Emerson expressed a similar opinion when he said: "We are to revise the whole of our social structure, the state, the school, religion, marriage, trade, science, and explore their foundations in our own nature.... Is it not the highest duty that man should be honored in us?"[6] In the face of complex, apparently unsolvable problems it is vital that we return to the starting point and remember our humanity.

The Passion of Linus Pauling

Krieger: Another great scientist who signed the Russell-Einstein Manifesto is Linus Pauling. Like Einstein and Rotblat, Pauling was outspoken in opposing nuclear weapons testing and in advocating their abolition. In 1957, he and his wife, Ava Helen, organized a petition among scientists to seek an end to atmospheric testing of nuclear weapons. It started as a petition of American scientists only but, assuming a life of its own, ultimately included scientists from all over the world.

Pauling delivered the petition with more than nine thousand signatures to Dag Hammarskjold, then-UN secretary-general. For his efforts to halt atmospheric nuclear testing, Linus Pauling received the 1962 Nobel Peace Prize, his second Nobel award.

Ikeda: According to Pauling, both his scientific and peace achievements were fueled by his desire to save human beings from suffering.[7] In science, his spirit of inquiry was inexhaustible. Working for peace, his conviction was unyielding.

As you know, in September 1998, the SGI organized an exhibition in San Francisco called "Linus Pauling and the Twentieth Century" with the cooperation of Pauling's family. We envisioned it as a way of establishing guidelines for the twenty-first century based on the nobility of Pauling's life and ideas.

Krieger: I was impressed by the tremendous effort you devoted to the exhibit, which even included antagonistic letters Pauling received because of his work for peace.

Ikeda: A video at the exhibition, which seemed to make an especially strong impression on visitors, showed Pauling remaining staunch in the face of criticism and pressure from the government and the media.

Krieger: It is a sad commentary on our society that someone should be reviled for working toward a more peaceful, less dangerous world. But nationalism's grip on the twentieth century, which continues into the new century, makes such antagonism possible and sometimes prevalent. Pauling was certainly not alone in being unjustly criticized. In spite of his critics, however, and without hesitation, he spoke the truth as he saw it and stood firm for human dignity. This was the measure of his greatness.

Ikeda: In twentieth-century Japan, Tsunesaburo Makiguchi, the first president of the Soka Gakkai, and Josei Toda, the second president, both fought for peace and humanity. The Japanese militarist fascists of the time were invading other nations and violating human rights. Makiguchi and Toda courageously stood up against them. Originating in religious faith, their actions arose from their staunch desire to foster universal opposition to fascism, which threatened human dignity.

Josei Toda has been the source of all my own work for peace. I have inherited his spiritual attitudes, and my life is devoted to taking the struggle for peace to the whole world.

The Power of the People

Ikeda: Historically, the reformation of society has been accomplished through the power of people passionately striving to accomplish their vows and goals. But today, unfortunately, society seems profoundly impotent. People are convinced that the individual is powerless to change the prevailing situation. Confronted with day-to-day reality, sensitive people lose hope and shut themselves within their own small worlds. This strikes me as a major evil of our times.

Krieger: Making people aware of their power to change policies and governments presents an important challenge. Of course, people have always had this power, even as far back as ancient China, with its concept of the Mandate of Heaven. The Chinese people overthrew rulers who lost the Mandate of Heaven. More recently, we have witnessed popular movements break down the Berlin Wall and reunite Germany; dismantle the former Soviet Union and create democratic governments in its stead; replace communist governments throughout Eastern Europe; overcome apartheid in South Africa; and replace corrupt governments in places like the Philippines, Haiti and Indonesia. We are just beginning to see the emergence of a powerful popular movement for globalization — the movement for global democracy, including the democratization of the World Trade Organization. I believe that more such movements are on the way.

Ikeda: Arnold J. Toynbee, the renowned British historian, once said that, ultimately, it is "deeper, slower movements "[8] that create history. I am certain that the power and actions of ordinary people residing in the subcurrents of history constitute those quiet movements. But as you say, while popular movements have made spectacular progress on the national scale in the last decade and a half, global democracy has yet to emerge.

In July 1998, Boutros Boutros-Ghali, the former UN secretary-general, told me that, in the twenty-first century, no individual nation will be capable of solving international problems. Such problems will have to be addressed as global issues unsolvable within domestic frameworks. This, he insisted, is the nature of our times.

Krieger: Many of the most important problems we face today cross national borders, which modern technologies make entirely permeable. Borders cannot restrain serious pollution or disease. They cannot protect against missile attacks capable of destroying even the most powerful nations. On the positive side, borders are permeable to ideas spread through modern forms of communication, including satellite television, cellular telephones and the Internet. While modern technologies have expanded our problems from national to regional and global scales, they have also provided means by which we can work together to solve these problems.

Loyalty to All Humanity

Ikeda: Ironically, as the world becomes increasingly borderless, people's awareness remains largely constrained within their national borders. This is the key aspect of the issue.

Krieger: Yes, paradoxically, most people are still conditioned to give their loyalty to a nation in a time when such loyalty often impedes action for the good of humanity as a whole. Few national political leaders today espouse a vision of a world order that prohibits war and weapons of mass destruction, that upholds human rights for all peoples everywhere and that holds leaders accountable under international law for crimes against humanity.

Ikeda: The adoption in July 1998 of a treaty setting up the International Criminal Court—which you had long advocated—was of great significance. UN Secretary-General Kofi Annan described it as a gift of hope for future generations. But developing it into something truly effective demands the support of ordinary people.

Krieger: Most people don't yet know much, if anything, about the International Criminal Court. People do know, though, when they are being abused and, in spite of tremendous obstacles, can rise up against tyranny. This new court would be a way to hold leaders accountable for serious crimes. It strongly upholds the interests of ordinary people.

Ikeda: As globalization proceeds, we enter an age in which everybody's actions strongly influence everybody else. When we realize this, we can then alter our mindset and strive to build a global society of mutual coexistence and mutual prosperity. This will be done by going beyond devotion to the interests of the nation-state and devoting ourselves to the interests of all humanity. As Martin Luther King Jr. said, injustice anywhere is a threat to justice everywhere. The key to the solution is, in your terms, the imagination to care for others.

It is the empathizing heart or what Buddhists refer to when they talk about mercy.

Krieger: At no other time has that imagination been in greater demand than today. Most troubling to me about the state of the world is a currently pervasive sense of complacency and indifference among the well-to-do. This represents the diametric opposite of empathy and compassion. We have tremendous potential to make the world a more decent place. Global news networks using modern technologies inform us about what is happening all over the planet. In spite of this information, however, many people remain in a state of complacency. The modern equivalent of fiddling while Rome burns is people watching television sitcoms as suffering continues and global threats to human dignity mount.

Ikeda: It is necessary for each individual to look reality in the face, speak out and initiate action in his or her immediate surroundings. The worst thing we can do is to resign ourselves to believing we are helpless. Instead, all of us must come together and revise our outlook. As the German philosopher Karl Jaspers said: "We can enjoy the happiness of existence in the interim granted to us. But it is a last respite. Either we avert the deadly peril or prepare for the catastrophe.... Today we stand poised on the razor's edge. We have to choose: to plunge into the abyss of man's lostness, and the consequent extinction of all earthly life, or to take the leap to the authentic man and his boundless opportunities through self-transformation."[9]

Krieger: People in the most powerful countries seem not to grasp the dangers inherent in relying for security on weapons of mass destruction. The very nuclear-armed states that threaten others with such weapons are themselves threatened with similar massive destruction. Citizens of rich countries often remain indifferent to the suffering of citizens of poor countries. Little is done to reduce the disparity between the rich and the poor. Indeed, that disparity seems to be widening.

The biggest challenge is to awaken people everywhere to the dangers to humanity as a whole and to each individual. But encouraging people to act and demanding change are not easy tasks and may have to be carried out person to person. Such activities may be disheartening at times and certainly demand perseverance. A strong will, together with hope— driven by a powerful spirit—are supremely important.

CHAPTER TWO

From a Century of War to a Century of Peace

Ikeda: The twentieth century was an epoch of war and violence in which regard for the dignity of life diminished within children's minds. The ensuing culture of violence that threatens human dignity is not limited to certain nations but is rampant the world over. This is one of the gravest problems confronting us at the start of the twenty-first century.

It follows that moving from a war culture to a peace culture is our most important concern at the beginning of the twenty-first century. The United Nations has designated the first ten years of the new century (2001–2010) the International Decade for a Culture of Peace and Non-Violence for the Children of the World.

In summer 1999, the youth of the SGI-USA initiated dialogues and a petition movement to educate the public about nonviolence. The young people decided on this plan out of a desire to make the twenty-first a century of peace and respect for life. They undertook various creative measures for developing a grass-roots dialogue movement. Among them was the production of a video titled "Teaching Nonviolence." The petition cards they distributed, bearing the title "Victory Over Violence," contained the following three-part pledge:

1. I will value my own life.
2. I will respect all life.
3. I will inspire hope in others.

Throughout America, the response to their activities has been greater than the young people imagined. More important, the youth involved have learned a great deal and developed because of the experience.

Krieger: It is especially significant because the young people initiated it on their own accord in their desire to change our times.

Many people in the United States are now trying to determine what to do about the current level of violence, including the series of school shootings like the one that took place in Littleton, Colorado.[1] At no time has America stood in greater need of the philosophy of nonviolence. At the Nuclear Age Peace Foundation we initiated a curriculum for high school students on human rights and responsibilities based on the Universal Declaration of Human Rights. When human rights are respected and upheld, violence is greatly diminished.

The pledge on the SGI-USA petition cards offers some important suggestions about individual responses to the grave social problem of violence. I agree with the young people who created this pledge: The basis for nonviolence is self-respect, which leads to respect for the dignity of each human being.

When young people take action they are bound to learn from their experience. It takes courage to speak out and act for nonviolence when surrounded by violence, but it is the only way to transform a culture of violence to a culture of peace.

Ikeda: True. The peace we seek cannot be brought about through a struggle for dominance in military or economic power. It can be won only through peaceful means. Peace built on the unhappiness and sacrifice of others is a meaningless sham. What's needed is to create a world in which people of all races and nations can enjoy peace and happiness.

Dialogue is the primary means. Though it may seem a roundabout process, dialogue is the surest way to open each available pathway to peace. It is impossible to move the human mind without employing dialogue in which communication takes place at the deepest level of life.

Socrates, a master of dialogue, immediately comes to mind in this connection.

Socrates, A Dangerous Gadfly?

Krieger: Indeed, dialogue was at the heart of Socrates' means of knowing and teaching. He sought to reveal the truth through dialogue and was not content until he did so. Because of his method and his search for truth, he was considered a dangerous gadfly.

Ikeda: Socrates badgered the city-state to wake up the citizens. He severely criticized people who avoided reality or would not own up to their responsibilities. In *The Republic*, Plato has Socrates say, "[The escapist] goes his own way. He is like one who, in the storm of dust and sleet which the driving wind hurries along, retires under the shelter of a wall; and seeing the rest of mankind full of wickedness, he is content, if only he can live his own life and be pure from evil or unrighteousness, and depart in peace and good-will, with bright hopes."[2]

Undeniably, those who stay out of the bog of reality and remain quietly in their own world escape wounding. They are carefree and avoid criticism. But I am convinced that the truly profound and great human life can be lived only in a courageous struggle at the price of immense personal pain.

Krieger: Socrates was a beacon of light. He sought the truth and challenged the accepted wisdom of the time. He tried to educate others by asking penetrating questions. My father greatly admired Socrates and held him up as a role model when I was a child. I enjoyed reading about Socrates' willingness to ask challenging questions about the established social order. For this, his fellow Athenians accused him of corrupting the youth of the city. Perhaps when you and I seek to inspire world citizenship in young people and to instill allegiance to humanity in them, when we encourage them to challenge the basing of national security on weapons of mass destruction, we, too, can be accused of corrupting youth by directing their vision above and beyond the borders of their own countries.

Ikeda: Though perverse, it is common to criticize people who struggle for the future of humanity. As is well known, Socrates' insistence on crying out for justice resulted in his premature death. Saying, "The whole world should be at odds with me, and oppose me, rather than that I myself should be at odds with myself, and contradict myself,"[3] he chose to take the poison prepared for him and die.

Krieger: To be frank, I have always thought that Socrates should have accepted the advice of his friends to escape instead of drinking the hemlock. By taking the poison, he recognized the authority of the state as above his own understanding of what is right. I believe that individual conscience occupies a higher level of authority than that of the state. Socrates' final lesson should not have been to bow to the authority of the state when he knew that he had done nothing wrong. I wish he had lived for his principles in defiance of the state rather than dying for them. At any rate, Socrates certainly taught us to not remain detached from the problems of the world.

Ikeda: I feel, however, that his death was no defeat. His great spirit passed on to his disciple Plato, who further elaborated his mentor's concepts of justice. That is why, still today, Socrates' life and philosophy continue to be beacons. The enduring image of Socrates as the man of justice was possible only because of Plato's struggle.

Krieger: As you have mentioned, Plato immortalized the story of Socrates. There are always younger generations to learn from the words and actions of those who precede them. I also put great faith in young people. Inevitably the future is in their hands, and it is up to them to choose what that future will be. Empowering young people to realize their potential for creating a just world is a goal worth fighting for regardless of criticism and obstacles. Achieving it is the duty of citizens of earth. I think Socrates would approve.

Growing Stronger Through Hardships

Ikeda: For a person of action, the words *regardless of criticism and obstacles* carry great weight. In your long work for peace, what has caused you the greatest suffering?

Krieger: My greatest suffering has often come from the walls of complacency I have faced. But my most difficult times have also been the times of greatest growth.

Ikeda: That insight strikes a chord with me. Since my youth, one of my mottoes has been: "Waves grow stronger the more obstacles they encounter."

Krieger: What matter are determination and persistence. In my own difficult times, I have looked to the words of great individuals like Mahatma Gandhi, Martin Luther King Jr. and Albert Camus to sustain me. For more than thirty years I have treasured this quotation by John F. Kennedy: "We must face the truth that the people have not been horrified by war to a sufficient extent to force them to go to any extent rather than have another war.... War will exist until the distant day when the conscientious objector enjoys the same reputation and prestige as the warrior does today."[4]

In my struggles, I have been sustained by a loving wife and children. They have stood by me throughout my life's journey for peace. I have been very fortunate to have their support.

Ikeda: That is wonderful. Many people talk about peace, but few really do anything about it. Very few are willing to fight the battle to the end. Josei Toda instilled in me the hard and fast rule that, even if we stand alone, we must never give up but must see the struggle through to its conclusion.

The year before he died, he said something I have never forgotten for a minute: "If we don't fight, justice will be defeated. Because justice is on our side, we must not lose. We absolutely must win. That's why we fight. The lion is most lionlike when he roars."

Krieger: Each generation is charged with renewing the fight for justice and for peace. And I believe these words of your mentor hold great importance for anyone choosing to take action for peace.

My work in the name of a peaceful, just world has brought me great happiness. Every day I am grateful for the opportunity to do work that I consider necessary. I am glad, too, for the chances I have of coming into contact and making close ties with young people. I am proud of helping to form the Nuclear Age Peace Foundation because it has much greater possibilities than I as an individual could have for realizing a world of peace and respect for human dignity.

What in your own extensive work for peace has brought you the greatest pain?

Ikeda: As might be expected, constant misunderstanding and slanderous criticism have caused me continual pain. Still, the supreme pride I take in being Josei Toda's disciple enables me to overcome everything. He constantly and forcefully insisted that the Soka Gakkai's mission is to bring lasting happiness to ordinary people on a scale not of centuries but of millennia. As his disciple, I have persevered with the same conviction that any moment could be my last. I live, leaving no regrets over actions not taken for the sake of peace.

The prejudices and unreasonable criticism addressed to my comrades in the pacifist struggle are more painful than anything said about me personally. Finding such unjust treatment intolerable, I have vowed to put myself in the front lines where I can shelter others. I have struggled against the odds and suffered for it, but this pain has become part of my life's golden record.

A Source of Paramount Happiness

Krieger: On what occasions have you experienced the greatest happiness?

Ikeda: Whenever I felt I was realizing my mentor's ideas. These were the times when my companion workers were happy for the same reason. Although he died more than forty years ago, I have cherished everything my mentor said and have nurtured plans for materializing his conviction that humanity can be brought together through peace, culture and education. The

Soka schools, Soka University and the Toda Institute for Global Peace and Policy Research are all realizations of his ideas. My having faithfully followed the disciple's way is a source of paramount happiness.

Other sources of irreplaceable joy include seeing friends whom I have encouraged overcome hardship and find happiness, and seeing the young people I have believed in and watched over grow and assume their extensive and active roles in the twenty-first century.

The Importance of a Mentor in Youth

Ikeda: Speaking of mentors — when the French philosopher Alain[5] was a youth, the guidance his mentor gave him contributed greatly to the development of his activism, which superseded his intellect in his later years. Once while participating in a nationwide high-school contest, Alain was required to write about justice. Since he was proficient in rhetoric, he considered this a very easy task. As he began writing, he caught the eye of his mentor, Jules Lagneau, who was monitoring the contest. Alain thought, "He'll be pleased if I write something good." But the look in his mentor's eyes was sterner than usual, which Alain sensed was telling him: "You don't know anything about this topic. Don't just write whatever comes into your head."

Lagneau had avoided teaching about justice, which he felt required action instead of mere words. Sensing his teacher's meaning, Alain changed his mind and wrote three impromptu sonnets on his test paper.

Krieger: Your story suggests several important lessons. It demonstrates the importance of a good teacher to a young person's development. Alain was fortunate, as you were, to have such a teacher. Also, it highlights the importance of self-restraint. It is sometimes better to say nothing when one has nothing significant to say. Ultimately, the story reminds us that justice demands action — that words, while based on thought and understanding, must at least suggest the possibility of action. In matters of justice we are tested not by artificial classroom examinations but by our actions in life.

Ikeda: As you say, having a trustworthy person who can guide you in life is a great blessing. Alain called Lagneau the only great man he ever met and his only mentor. I understand how he felt. I can positively declare that I owe everything I am today to the more than ten years during which Josei Toda trained me.

Krieger: Great teachers are also fortunate to find dedicated and talented students.

Concrete Proposals Spark the Light of Peace

Ikeda: Toda, who pioneered inquiries into the philosophy of peace with such works as his Declaration for the Abolition of Nuclear Weapons, repeatedly told me, "It is important to make concrete proposals toward the peace of humankind and to take the lead in seeing them realized." He also said that concrete proposals — even if they are not immediately realized — become the sparks from which the light of peace will grow. Empty talk is futile. The concreteness of a proposal is the pillar of its realization, which supports the roof protecting humanity.

Engraved deep in the substance of my young life, Toda's teachings were the objects of my study and contemplation during every available minute. All the many proposals —

including those for peace, which I have issued every year since 1983—were born of this contemplation. In addition, I have worked earnestly to implement the ideas I have proposed. I believe it is important to maintain high ideals while letting actions demonstrate our concrete policies for attaining peace.

Krieger: Your proposals fulfill an important responsibility to humanity. They demonstrate a clear understanding of the serious problems confronting us. Instead of stopping at observation, they educate and enlighten toward a popular awareness and summon people to action. This sort of vision and consistency of word and deed can change the world.

Dialogue and Action

Ikeda: As you point out, powerful popular solidarity is essential to actual reform. Cultivating solidarity among the people as a force for lasting peace has been the goal of my worldwide travels. As I mentioned, although it may seem a modest method, dialogue is the only thing with the power to generate soul-stirring encounters that truly change humanity. The longest journey begins with the first step. I am convinced that the highway to peace can be opened by repeated dialogue. Striving to apply this conviction, I have worked to expand a network of good people throughout the world by conversing and making friends with everyone, regardless of nationality or race, on the basis of our shared humanity.

Krieger: Dialogue provides an important way to expand our understanding of the world. Through dialogue, we can engage in reasoned discourse with people of diverse perspectives and experience.

The centerpiece of the intellectual activity of the Center

for the Study of Democratic Institutions, where I spent two years in the early 1970s, was dialogue. Some fifteen to twenty people of different academic disciplines would come together to discuss critical issues. The backgrounds of the participants were not sufficiently diverse, however. This meant that many important perspectives failed to reach the discussion table and thus failed to enter the discourse.

Ikeda: In other words, because of excessive similarity of attitude and approach, the creativity inherent in dialogue was less apparent than had been hoped?

Krieger: Yes. It is important for dialogue to cross cultural boundaries. I know that you have made a point of doing this.

I agree with you that dialogues are good starting points for approaching difficult problems. Even when they don't directly provide answers, they promote mutual understanding by shedding light on difficult problems, thus bringing them into focus.

Happiness Is Being Engaged With the World

Ikeda: I'm curious to know what has encouraged you most and made you happiest in your work for peace.

Krieger: I have been encouraged because the world has changed in important ways. The number of international wars has diminished. Progress has been made toward banning biological and chemical weapons. There has been some progress toward nuclear disarmament but far from enough. Many dictatorships have given way to more democratic governance. These are all positive signs. They are not sufficient, but they also are not insignificant.

The world cannot go on as it is now. I want to see the

nuclear threat to humanity ended, and I want to see an end to warfare as a means of settling disputes. These cannot be achieved by words alone. That is why I have pushed for action. I am happiest when I am fully engaged and when I can see even small signs of progress.

Ikeda: The times are indeed changing. Shortly after the end of World War II, when the ideological confrontation that led to the Cold War was heating up, Josei Toda proposed the idea of global citizenship. Many people laughed it off as a mere dream. Now, however, transcending racism and nationalism has become a pressing global issue.

It is mere complacency to simply accept the status quo believing change is "unrealistic." People relinquish their ability to make sound judgments when they think that what has been impossible up till now will remain impossible. It is crucial to realize that reform is an imperative and to act.

In the past, people have dispensed with such harmful and useless institutions as slavery and apartheid. There is no reason we cannot dispense with armaments, too. Riding a global wave of public opinion, the International Treaty to Ban Landmines was concluded in only a year. The elimination of nuclear weapons is not impossible. It is up to us to blaze the way.

Krieger: This is my intention, my goal and my greatest desire. It is possible, and it is necessary if we are to secure humanity's future. I believe it is the greatest challenge of our time and represents a true turning point for all humanity. We have no choice but to act on this most critical issue.

CHAPTER THREE

The Challenge
To Bring Forth a New Reality

Ikeda: Participants in peace movements are often criticized as fanciful and unrealistic. But distinctions between realistic and unrealistic are usually imposed arbitrarily by self-proclaimed realists.

Krieger: People who see themselves as realists tend to have limited vision at best. They often view the world and human nature as nasty and brutish, as did the English philosopher Thomas Hobbes. They believe that the proper response to the human condition is power and more power. Because they have little hope for societal transformation, such realists are often eager to use societal resources for military purposes and to rely upon sophisticated weapons, including weapons of mass destruction, for protection. The worst realists are cynical. They use their view of the human condition as a pretext to further their own agendas while letting the problems of society grow worse and the poorest of the poor sink deeper into misery.

I find the realist view very narrow. It makes no allowances for the possibility of creating a more humane world and often dismisses people who seek change.

Ikeda: One tragedy of our times is the willingness of realists, in spite of impending crises, to criticize and obstruct people who expend their energy toward finding solutions. Their judgments, however, are superficial and conventional, and their attitude distances them from the essential quality of reality — change. Often the wisest realists cannot escape this trap. The challenge, then, is to create a new kind of reality that offers hope for changing the world.

Krieger: To those who see human nature as evil and untrustworthy, I say that, like our technologies, human beings have the potential for both good and evil. We are educable creatures. We can be educated to be mean and uncaring or compassionate and altruistic. Infants have the potential to develop in one direction or the other — it all depends upon their upbringing and education. Compassionate societies can be constructed when we raise our children with love and compassion.

Education Makes Us Human

Ikeda: Education allows us to be truly human. It deepens us and enables us to build a better society and a brighter future. The profundity of education determines the profundity of culture, the nature of society and the firmness of peace. As you say, education plays a major role in creating deep solidarity, mutual understanding and trust.

The Soka Gakkai has long associations with education. Our first two presidents — Tsunesaburo Makiguchi and Josei Toda, whom I mentioned earlier — were both educators, and our organization was originally named the Soka Kyoiku Gakkai, or Value-creating Education Society. In this tradition, I decided from the outset that education would be one of my most important areas of focus. The development of a humane educational system led me to establish such institutions as Soka University and the Soka elementary, junior and senior high schools.

Krieger: In my view, idealists are needed now more than ever. They point the way to a better future. They show the possibility of changing our thinking, as Einstein warned we must do. Peace activists are often more strongly motivated by idealism and hope than by projections of present trends into the future. Hope makes change possible. It breaks down the barriers realism imposes. It opens the door on a future that is generous and decent instead of simply a projection of the past.

Ikeda: How limited is people's concept of reality. Napoleon was shocked to learn that the kingdom of Ryukyu possessed no armaments of any kind. He had thought the idea of a totally unarmed state inconceivable. That was back in 1816, but even today there are nations such as Costa Rica that maintain no armaments.

Krieger: Costa Rica provides a valuable example. It has demonstrated that a nation can survive and prosper without an army. People today who cannot imagine a world free of nuclear weapons are the reason progress toward eliminating those weapons has stalled even though the Cold War has ended.

Revival of the Imagination

Ikeda: Instead of being engrossed in transient "reality," humanity requires a revival of imagination to serve as a bridge connecting reality and ideals, as a source of hope. John F. Kennedy never resigned himself to accepting the impossibility of peace or the extinction of the human race. Instead he called out for the power to pioneer a better fate for humankind. In June 1963, he said: "Too many of us think [peace] is impossible. Too many think it unreal. But that is a dangerous, defeatist belief. We need not accept that view. Our problems are manmade — therefore, they can be solved by man."[1]

You have said that the line between reality and imagination depends on the viewpoint and attitude of the definer. You added that, with the support of the people, ideals become reality.

Krieger: Yes. In many instances, our understanding of reality is determined by our perspective. I can imagine two kinds of future for humanity — a very positive one and a very bleak one. The positive future would build on a culture of peace. Human beings would treat one another with respect and compassion. All people would be educated to fulfill their potential. Such a future would provide ways for all human beings to live with dignity. We would be good stewards of our planet and its resources for succeeding generations.

Ikeda: I believe that — little by little — that sort of society is already forming.

Krieger: True, but I can also imagine a future that is like hell on earth. In it, we would destroy our planet by plundering its resources and polluting the air and water essential to health and life itself. We would continually fight over dwindling resources. Abounding ethnic, religious and national hatreds would fuel a culture of militarism and war.

The poor would become poorer. Their lives, as Hobbes suggested, would be nasty, brutish and short. While growing richer, the rich would become insular and fearful of war and environmental pollution. New diseases and plagues would continually

threaten survival. Hope itself would become increasingly re-
mote. For some people, this future is already their present.

I believe our world will move in the direction of one or the
other of these two imagined futures. By our actions now, we
will collectively choose our direction. Indeed, our orientation
toward the future is one of the most important choices facing
humanity — and each of us individually.

Good and Evil: Two Aspects of the Human Mind

Ikeda: Buddhism teaches that human life is endowed simultane-
ously with both good and evil. The human mind is interpreted
as partaking of ten different conditions, or states, including, at
one end of the scale, Hell, which is filled with suffering;
Hunger, dominated by greed; and Animality, characterized by
fear of the strong and contempt for the weak. At the other end
are the Bodhisattva and Buddha conditions — states of mind in
which people strive to help others by eliminating suffering and
imparting happiness. Buddhism further teaches that the nature
of life is for good and evil to be essentially inseparable.

Krieger: It seems that good and evil do exist side by side in our
world. There is always tension between them.

Ikeda: The self and the other are always capable of either good
or bad. We can cultivate self-control and find ways to improve
when we conduct a ceaseless spiritual struggle to discover
what is evil in one's self and what is good in others.

The terrorist attacks of September 11, 2001, serve as a tragic
example of this, an ultimate manifestation of evil that shows us
the vilest depths to which human nature can sink. While it is
impossible not to be outraged at the senseless loss of so many
lives, in the end, the evil over which we must triumph is the

impulse toward hatred and destruction that resides in us all. Unless we can perceive our fellow human beings and feel their sufferings as our own, we will never be free of conflict and war. In other words, a transformation within our own lives is important.

The Buddhist teaching of the inseparability of evil and good means that everything can be made one or the other in an instant, according to what we harbor in our hearts. Everything begins with the self. A change in one's outlook or intention triggers a change in the self and radiates outward to effect society-wide revolutions. This idea is what we in the SGI refer to as "human revolution."

As you say, humankind can follow a path leading to a bleak future, but that course is not inevitable.

Krieger: Certainly it is not. We must not allow tragedy to repeat itself. But merely choosing the path of peace is not enough. To move in that direction demands that we work diligently, that we commit ourselves to the path of peace and do our utmost to encourage others to join in this effort. If we fail, we may follow the path leading to a dark future. If we simply follow what is probably the path of least resistance, humankind may once again be engulfed in an era of tragedy.

Human Revolution: The Path to a Hopeful Future

Ikeda: In short, we need preparedness and enthusiasm for the struggle to convert ideals into reality. The Argentine writer Julio Cortázar said: "We must make reality conform to our dreams. We must eliminate the boundaries between the fictional and the concrete. We must realize ourselves and go on dreaming until we find that paradise lost is there and that we have turned all corners."[2]

Ideals are not far removed. Once people can regain their essential humanity, we will find that we have "turned all corners." Cortázar's words are in keeping with our ideal of human revolution.

Krieger: Making reality conform to our dreams is a serious challenge. Social structures preventing people from realizing their dreams cause much of the sadness and emptiness in the world. Some human structures, particularly brutal authoritarian regimes, even try to foreclose the possibility of dreaming. In subtler ways, consumer societies replace authentic human dreams with desires for commercial products.

Ikeda: Unspeakable regimes that try to forbid people even to dream will eventually crumble, like the militarist dictatorships of Latin America in the 1980s and Eastern European regimes somewhat later. In consumer societies, the danger is submerged. Nonetheless, it is serious, as it obscures true ideals. Václav Havel, playwright, philosopher and president of the Czech Republic, warns that hedonists buried in a consumer society are like domestic cattle. Their lives are devoid of meaning.

"Such people," wrote Havel, "cease being responsible for themselves and their lives — inevitably they lose awareness of their autonomous personalities and dignity and become lumps of mud completely dependent on belonging to the entire bog." That is why restoring our reason for living and putting hope back in the human heart are supremely important.

Krieger: It is important to encourage young people to embrace the ideal of creating a better future for themselves and all humanity. The challenge is to build societies in which individuals have optimum possibilities for realizing their dreams.

As I understand it, Cortázar's concept of turning all corners means that to find worthy ideals entails a struggle and that the struggle itself will teach us who we really are.

Sowing Seeds of Peace

Ikeda: If we struggle continuously with reality, without fleeing from it, we will awaken to our true selves, a goal toward which Buddhism emphasizes action. As a concrete method of actualizing ideals, your Nuclear Age Peace Foundation advocates "Sowing Seeds of Peace."

Krieger: I think sowing seeds of peace is a very important concept. In a sense, it is what remains after we realize we cannot change the world by our desire alone. I have seen many people try to change the world with one dramatic action. Such people are often very enthusiastic and filled with goal-oriented energy. The problem is that no single event or activity is ever enough. When they see that — in spite of their hard work — the world has not changed in any dramatic way, they are frequently disappointed and give up. It is a great loss when, as I have repeatedly seen, energetic people give up rather than continue to sow seeds of peace.

Ikeda: Gandhi said, "Good travels at a snail's pace."[3] The peace movement cannot accomplish things radically and all at once. Often, it can only advance by gradual and protracted means. Gradualism does not, however, imply negative compromise or merely passing time. It means truly reforming our times by sowing seeds of peace in individual minds through sincere dialogue and, in this way, cultivating consensus.

Only the courageous and persevering can be gradualists. Though it may seem roundabout, this is the road to the creation of peace.

Krieger: As you say, sowing seeds of peace demands persever-ance. Once planted, the seeds require nurturing and, only later, can the harvest be reaped. In other words, the peace process requires sustained commitment. Those who work to sow seeds of peace always seek new ways to reach out and to find fertile ground for planting.

Ikeda: That is what I had in mind when, at the inception of the SGI in 1975, I urged my audience to devote their precious lives less to personal success than to sowing seeds of peace all over the world.

Krieger: That is a way to give greater meaning to one's life. If commitment is to be long-term, peace itself must be the goal. Finding satisfaction in the work itself and in struggling to over-come obstacles is imperative for people dedicated to building a better, more peaceful world.

Unflagging Optimism

Ikeda: Unflagging optimism in the face of everything and any-thing, and a deep trust in the power of the people provide the driving force behind gradualism.

The noted pacifist scholar Johan Galtung tells young peo-ple, "We must be realists in our brains while keeping the flame of idealism burning in our hearts."[4] Both of these — to see the world as it is and how it could be — are essential to reform. A firm hold on reality should not entail being swamped by or resting easy in the status quo. To pioneer uncharted ways requires that people today keep the lamp of optimism lit.

Krieger: I appreciate very much your concept of unflagging optimism. We must *choose* optimism; in doing so, we are also choosing hope. But, even for the most dedicated individual, staying optimistic sometimes requires great psychological struggle. In spite of our desire to believe that justice and right will prevail, life teaches us that often they do not. Injury and suffering are inflicted on many people, and even the law is not always just. Consequently, unflagging optimism requires discipline and commitment.

Ikeda: How can people break with the so-called realistic approach and live for their ideals?

Krieger: It is primarily a matter of conviction and determination. First, of course, people need ideals they believe are worth fighting for. They also require the faith that creating a better world is possible. To break from the realistic approach also entails breaking the chains of complacency. None of this is easy, but each person who lives this way becomes an example, a teacher, for others. We can never know for certain whom our lives influence, but we can be certain that living in accord with our ideals will have an effect on others.

The Power of Education

Ikeda: The tragedy of war becomes inevitable unless people have the power to prevent authority from running amok. This is why individuals need wisdom, strength and a sense of solidarity.

Krieger: Creating societies in which individuals exhibit wisdom, strength and solidarity is quite a challenge. Essentially, it is a matter of education. In such societies, the leaders would also reflect these characteristics and would, therefore, not need to be bridled. Most societies today, however, are far from this ideal. For this reason, critical and independent thinking should be cultivated as an important component of education. People who think critically can challenge accepted assumptions and reach conclusions on the basis of logic and their own understanding of various factors. Thinking independently requires confidence in one's own reasoning abilities. One role of education is to cultivate this kind of self-confidence.

During the Vietnam War, a bumper sticker saying "Question Authority" was popular in the United States. Its underlying message was that people should think for themselves and not go along with the illegal and immoral war being perpetrated by the political authorities.

Ikeda: Josei Toda warned us to keep a cautious eye on politics. He also insisted that education is the driving power to orient political leaders, who are prone to arbitrary authoritarianism, toward the good of ordinary people and humanity. In the past, desiring to keep the people easily manageable, political authorities deprived them of educational opportunities. Even now, when such opportunities are available, authorities often limit instruction to that which ensures loyalty and suppresses independent thought.

Despots fear education and want to keep the people ignorant and submissive. Religions that wish to keep the people under their control also dread the power of education and, as history shows, have been known to oppress committed teachers. Without education, people can easily be enslaved to political and religious authority. The more deceived the people, the more high-handed the authorities. This vicious circle must be broken.

Krieger: I concur completely. In societies where people are educated to think for themselves and keep a watchful eye on their leaders, leaders find it far harder to be oppressive and tyran-nical. Through critical thinking in our daily lives, we can chal-lenge authority when necessary.

Of course, this is much harder to do under authoritarian and repressive regimes. In such circumstances, it is necessary for the international community to step in and prevent abuses of the rights of those who would challenge authority.

CHAPTER FOUR

Peace
Leadership

Ikeda: Because thoughtful people always ponder the issue of war and peace, many peace movements have arisen. Some have been masks for authority to hide behind. Others have been means to satisfy specific interests, and still others have performed in ways inconsistent with their professed high aims. Some movements have lost sight of their initial lofty ideals, gradually deteriorating over time.

Peace movements cannot achieve their aims overnight— they take plenty of time and effort. But fundamentally they require the autonomous action of each participant. Consequently, more than anything else, staying power determines the success or failure of a peace movement.

Krieger: Yes, individual perseverance is essential to accomplishing any important goal. All authentic peace movements are committed to long-term efforts. After all, peace is a process that must continually be renewed. Opposing the forces of violence embedded in current national systems and in relations between nations requires courage and long-term commitment.

Ikeda: To bear fruit, a peace movement absolutely requires clear vision and leaders of unshakable convictions and passion. I have been convinced of this from conversations with the leaders of numerous peace movements including the Pugwash Conferences and International Physicians for the Prevention of Nuclear War. I consider it important for leaders to be imbued with the willingness to lay down their lives for their ideals. As history teaches, movements whose leaders lose their resolve stagnate and ultimately decline. In contrast, though it may take time, movements ultimately attain their goals as long as their leaders' minds are aflame with their convictions.

Krieger: Many social forces, though, may try to wear down and discredit such leaders. Great peace leaders have paid the ultimate price for their commitment to creating more just and peaceful societies. Gandhi and King were assassinated. So were Egyptian President Anwar Sadat and Israeli Prime Minister Yitzhak Rabin for trying to lead the way to peace in the Middle East.

Ikeda: Gandhi's nonviolence movement stands as one of the most brilliant achievements of the twentieth century. He said that what one person can do, everyone can do. His actions brought courage and hope to ordinary people. Though at a glance his movement seems reckless, it succeeded. Why? Kafka provided a hint.

Upon hearing that the British authorities had arrested Gandhi, Kafka said: "This makes it clear that Gandhi's movement will win. Putting him in jail enables his party to make big advances. Any movement without a martyr falls victim to the interests of speculators interested in nothing but success. Their rushing currents end up puddles where all hope for the future rots. This is because the *idée*—like all things with super-personal value in this world—lives only on personal sacrifices."

Peace Must Be Won Each Day

Krieger: I wonder if doing what one is convinced is right can correctly be viewed as a sacrifice. I believe that for individuals to advance the cause of peace demands great conviction and perseverance. Peace cannot be won easily. Nor does one victory guarantee that it will last. Peace is won on an almost daily basis. In the end, it is not simply a matter of reaching an accord to refrain from violence. Peace is something that ultimately resides in the human heart, guiding individual behavior and providing support for just and peaceful public policy — particularly foreign policy.

Ikeda: I fully understand what you mean. More than two hundred years ago, Kant wrote that, ultimately, eternal peace means limitless, continual advancement toward the goal. Endless striving is the only way to realize peace. Negligence resulting from over-confidence and satisfaction invites peril. Peace, once achieved, does not last forever by itself. It requires vigilance throughout all the activities of daily life.

Krieger: Since I view peace in the same broad way, I see it as a lifetime commitment and a way of life. It is the work I consciously choose and try to succeed at each day. This is my kind of leadership. I try to stimulate others to join in working for peace. But, since talents and abilities differ, I encourage each person to find his or her own way to contribute to the building of a peaceful world. I am convinced that we all share the responsibility for this task — a responsibility to ourselves, to our families and communities, to future generations and to the earth.

Our Collective Responsibility for Peace

Ikeda: That is an important point. No one person can achieve the goal alone. To effect reform requires us to pool our minds and strengths. Each flower has its own kind of beauty. And Buddhism teaches that society is enriched when each person brings his or her individuality to full blossom.

From another viewpoint, it is highly important to cultivate in each person what Gandhi called the fearless mind. As long as a person is determined to contribute to peace and to tolerate no injustice, there is no point in worrying about the manner in which he or she participates in the work. Indeed, solidarity is broader and more flexible and movements more enduring when optimum use is made of each participant's individuality.

Krieger: That is true. Personally, I give highest priority to abolishing nuclear weapons. But it makes sense for people in war zones or places where human rights are abused or where extreme poverty persists to give top priority to solving problems confronting them directly.

Even after we have abolished nuclear weapons, we will certainly not have achieved a peaceful world. Much will remain to be done for the cause of peace; nonetheless, eliminating nuclear weapons is a critical step forward. My advice to people who want to promote the cause of peace is to never give up and to work knowing that the future of the world depends on what each of us does. We are all participants in creating the future.

Ikeda: It takes the initiative of ordinary individuals to eliminate nuclear weapons and create a peaceful world. This certainty entails a profound sense of responsibility. Tackling global problems demands that we cultivate in ourselves the same mettle and conviction as that of the heroes of historical reformation.

The Nuclear Age Peace Foundation is an influential non-governmental organization. What did you feel were the most important issues when you and your colleagues founded it?

Building the Nuclear Age Peace Foundation

Krieger: The key issue on our minds was the extreme danger to humanity in the Nuclear Age. The principal danger is the existence and threat of nuclear weapons, but other technologies are also threatening. It was and remains our conviction that peace is an imperative of the Nuclear Age. Another danger is the complacency of most people toward the threat of nuclear annihilation. We wanted to help shake people out of complacency and inspire them to act.

We realized we were making a long-term commitment to build an organization that would work for peace in many ways and to not give up. We knew there was no single approach. In fact, assuming the opposite, we saw that many approaches were needed to discover what works best. Most important, we knew it would take time to achieve our goals. We did not want to be sprinters but long-distance runners. From the outset, we have looked to the future and have tried to increase our credibility and effectiveness with each step forward.

Ikeda: Since I, too, consider the building of peace a desperate battle, I can imagine the pains you've undergone while nurturing your Foundation. Josei Toda always told me to regard each small matter as substantial and to work constantly to build all-important credibility. "Once you have credibility," he said, "everything else will open up for you."

The bigger the goal, the more time and effort it takes to

attain. This is why you boldly adopted the attitude of the long-distance runner. Instead of striving for short-term results, you have resolved to move step by step toward the building of peace, gaining credibility as you go. Your organization is still permeated by your original resolution.

Krieger: Today our Foundation is active in many fields. We work daily to abolish nuclear weapons, to strengthen international law and institutions, and to build an enduring legacy of peace through education and advocacy. We publish our "Waging Peace" newsletter and a series of *Waging Peace* booklets and books. We also publish a free electronic newsletter, "The Sunflower." We reach out to many different groups in many different ways. We have a particular interest in reaching out to young people. We offer internships for college students and conduct an annual international peace essay contest for highschool students. We offer prizes for peace poetry in different age categories. We have created a peace garden in a beautiful natural environment on the grounds of a retreat center in Santa Barbara, where each year the anniversaries of Hiroshima and Nagasaki are commemorated. In addition, we have many peace education projects, including projects on peace heroes and on the history of the Nuclear Age. We developed a special curriculum on human rights and responsibilities based on the Universal Declaration of Human Rights. We also have a project on inspiring hope for the future, including a lecture series on ideas for shaping the future.

Ikeda: All these are splendid undertakings. The importance of peace education is certain to increase in the coming years. Projects honoring peace heroes have great symbolic significance for the transition from a culture of war to a culture of peace.

In my travels around the world, I have noticed that though

statues to war heroes abound, statues or memorial plaques to heroes of peace and humanity are rare. The spiritual environment that has resulted in this situation needs to be reformed.

The task is to make peace and humanitarian concern the dominant spirit of the age and the fertile spiritual soil for the culture of peace.

Krieger: We have significantly increased the Foundation's audience through the Internet. I am very pleased we can now reach people and spread our ideas all over the world electronically.[1] We also try to network constructively and cooperate with like-minded organizations throughout the world.

Nongovernmental Organization Solidarity

Ikeda: Solidarity among a large number of NGOs has recently produced some startling results—for example, the World Court Project brought the topic of the illegality of nuclear weapons to the International Court of Justice, and the International Campaign to Ban Landmines dramatically achieved its goal.

Krieger: Powerful backing from NGOs added strength and impetus to both the movements you mention and also to the movement to establish an International Criminal Court. No doubt networking of this kind will be essential in attaining other truly important goals such as the elimination of nuclear weapons. Lasting peace itself will only be achieved by creating a fabric of institutional structures based on underlying attitudes supporting nonviolent means of resolving conflicts. Even after they have been created, however, such institutions will require the support and encouragement of people throughout the world because there will probably always be forces working against their survival.

Exchanges with individuals and organizations have taught me the importance of remaining hopeful. We can never be certain what will lead to the breakthroughs we seek. But, if we keep working toward our goals in a steady, determined way, we may succeed as others have before us. And, even if we fall short of our goals, the messages of hope we send out will inspire others.

PART TWO

PERSONAL MOTIVATIONS
FOR PEACE ACTIVISM

CHAPTER FIVE

Children
of the Nuclear Age

Ikeda: No one can deny that the twentieth has been a century of war. Extraordinary violence and revolution dominated the first half. Humanity was compelled to suffer the misery of two world wars. In the latter half of the century, the dark, ominous cloud of the Nuclear Age descended, a predicament reflected in the name of your Foundation. The emergence of nuclear weapons has confronted humanity with a bleak new horizon.

Krieger: The novelist Kurt Vonnegut described the first and second world wars as humankind's first and second attempts to commit collective suicide. Clearly there was madness and self-destructiveness in these wars, as there is in all warfare. Nonetheless, until the middle of the twentieth century, we lacked the capacity to destroy ourselves completely. Now, with arsenals of thermonuclear weapons, we have that capacity. This is the basis of Einstein's famous comment that with the splitting of the atom, everything has changed save our modes of thinking. Unfortunately, the madness in human thinking that motivated the terrible world wars of the twentieth century persists.

Ikeda: In February 1999, the American media museum, the Newseum, compiled a list of the hundred top news items of the twentieth century. In it, the bombings of Hiroshima and Nagasaki took first place ahead of other momentous events such as the landing of human beings on the moon and the Wright brothers' first flight. This suggests how decisive the emergence of nuclear weapons has been for human history.

Krieger: When my colleagues and I created our organization in 1982, we spent many hours discussing what to call it. We settled on the Nuclear Age Peace Foundation because we felt that the Nuclear Age represents a critical historical break with the past and that, in this new period, *peace is an imperative.* Peace is no longer merely preferable; it is essential if we are to survive as a species.

Ikeda: It is unfortunate, however, that political leaders all over the world cannot break with outmoded security notions even though the Cold War, which arose directly out of the existence of nuclear arms, has ended. They insist on security for the state instead of human security.

The Deterrence Myth

Krieger: Very few political leaders have been innovative in the search for peace. The political process in most countries — particularly most industrialized countries — weeds out visionary leaders. Leaders are elected on the basis of what it is perceived they can do for their country: whether they can generate greater prosperity and security. Of course, those are good things. But, in keeping with the old paradigm, most politicians pursue them for their own countries at the expense of other countries. They do not understand that the prosperity and security of all countries are interdependent. Global prosperity and security — like global peace — are indivisible. Mikhail Gorbachev was one of the rare political leaders who had a vision of how to end the nuclear-weapons era.

Ikeda: Although he could have remained a superpower leader sequestered in the depths of the Kremlin, Gorbachev chose the path that led to the end of the Cold War. Knowing perfectly well that if he broke the dike the torrent of the revolution he unleashed would sweep him away, he nonetheless forged ahead.[1]

His great achievement was to smash the bedrock of the Cold War system at a time when an individual's power was considered insignificant. Because of this very important fact, I see hope for a world free of nuclear weapons.

Krieger: Years after the end of the Cold War, the leaders of nuclear-weapons states hang on to these weapons in the name of national security. In fact, instead of safety, they offer only the threat of mutual destruction, in which there is no security, only murder on an unprecedented scale with the possibility of human annihilation.

Ikeda: The policy of nuclear deterrence is just an excuse to justify nuclear weapons. In the industrialized world, peace through nuclear deterrence is bought at the price of hot wars in the developing world. Events in Korea, Vietnam and Afghanistan clearly reveal the impossibility of proving that nuclear weapons deter warfare. When accepting the Nobel Peace Prize, Joseph Rotblat asked how many more wars were required to overturn the deterrence argument. Looking back on a century of fear and death, his comment strikes an especially foreboding note.

Krieger: Wars in the poorer parts of the world and the impending threat of nuclear holocaust underline the need for peace. For people who believe life is sacred, allowing a few countries to put the future of humanity and most other forms of life in jeopardy of annihilation is intolerable. It makes no sense. Yet this is today's reality. Too little is being done to end this overarching threat of nuclear annihilation.

The Tramp of Military Boots

Ikeda: Because of my experience with war, I resolved to devote my life to the cause of world peace. At the time of Japan's defeat in World War II, I was seventeen. You might say that the tramp of military boots crushed my youth.

Militaristic education was wrong; but, during World War II, Japanese boys were patriotic enough to want to volunteer. I dreamed of becoming an aviator. When my father learned of this, he scolded me worse than he had ever done before or would ever do. "Not on your life!" he shouted. "Nothing will make me let them take my fifth boy away from me!" My four older brothers had already been drafted. The oldest was killed in action in Burma in 1945. When notification of his death came, I was sitting behind my mother. I couldn't see her face, but her back conveyed an unforgettable impression of grief.

The year my brother died, a downed American aviator parachuted to earth near my aunt's house. Japanese soldiers beat him with sticks and kicked him before the military police blindfolded him and took him away. When my mother heard about the incident, she expressed pity for the American and concern for *his* mother, who, she said, must be "so worried about him." Her words still echo in my ear.

Krieger: The loss of your brother must have left a void in your mother's heart, but it is clear that she did not lose her humanity.

Ikeda: War brought misery to our family and laid a heavy burden on me. Though suffering from tuberculosis, with all my brothers gone, I had to look after both my father and mother. In this phase of my life, I began entertaining doubt and anger about militaristic education. I saw the cruelty and futility of war.

The Influence of Josei Toda

Krieger: These wartime experiences must have opened your eyes and your heart to the importance of peace. I would like to hear more about how you became connected with the peace movement.

Ikeda: As I have said, the Soka Gakkai peace movement started with Makiguchi's and Toda's struggle against militarism. The militarists imprisoned both of them. Makiguchi died in prison. Toda was released after two years, though his health was thereafter impaired. He felt his mission was to take Buddhist humanism to the people of war-torn Japan. In spite of physical debility, he resolved to fulfill that mission. His struggle became the spiritual mainstay of our pacifist work.

By the time I met Josei Toda, I was already questioning the nature of true patriotism. I believed in him completely because he opposed war and because, though arrested under the infamous Peace Preservation Law, he continued his struggle against militarism. My decisive meeting with Toda was the start of my peace activities.

Krieger: How did you meet Toda?

Ikeda: It was in 1947, when I was nineteen and the whole nation had been ravaged by the war. With the collapse of the old system, all of us young people found ourselves compelled to revise our values and to search for something to fill our spiritual emptiness. Like many of my contemporaries, I sought meaning in life.

Despite my tuberculosis, I worked by day and went to night school. On one occasion, a member of a reading circle I belonged to told me about Soka Gakkai group meetings where people seriously discussed the philosophy of the force of life itself. At the first meeting I attended, I saw Toda casually lecturing to a poorly dressed but enthusiastic group. To all my inquiries he gave such sincere, straightforward, convincing answers that I knew he spoke the real truth. This conviction determined the rest of my life.

His explanations contained something universal. No matter what I asked, he satisfied me completely. As I learned more about him, I came to see that I was right—he always told the truth as it was. I decided that my life would be free of regrets if I followed him.

Krieger: A very powerful encounter. You are fortunate to have found such a mentor, and he was also fortunate to have found such a dedicated disciple in you.

Ikeda: We were only together for a brief ten-and-a-half years. Throughout that time, he devoted himself to guiding and educating me, though he knew the effort might shorten his life.

His business affairs were in a bad state at the time. Helping him rebuild them compelled me to stop attending night school. But from about 1950, he personally took charge of my education and almost every morning instructed me in a whole range of subjects including law, politics, economics, history, astronomy, Chinese literature and modern philosophy. I attended what might be called Toda University.

His greatest legacy to the world was his Declaration for the Abolition of Nuclear Weapons. To me personally, he taught the importance of dialogue. "We live in an age of dialogue," he said to me. "From now on, you're going to meet first-rate people on many occasions. Engage them in dialogue because, in dialogue, you put your whole personality on the line. That's why it's the best way to win real confidence."

As Toda clearly saw, confidence born of the personal contacts of dialogue is indispensable to the abolition of nuclear weapons.

Education in the Value of Life

Krieger: You were fortunate to receive that sort of education. In warfare, feelings of basic human decency are often suspended. War compels otherwise decent people to choose between killing and being killed. The choice is unreasonable, and forcing young people to make it is unjust. Young people lack a reference point with which to judge the education they receive. Nationalistic and militaristic education may be all they know.

They are likely to discover, however, that the actual cruelty and slaughter of war are very different from the fine things said about war in the classroom and in society. Your own conclusion about war's terrible reality was based on suffering you witnessed. A culture that infuses education with nationalism and militarism is a failed culture.

Ikeda: Such education does not deserve the name. It runs counter to the future of youth and human happiness. War is the direct antithesis of culture.

Krieger: The only worthy education teaches young people the sacredness of life—a gift we share with some six billion other human beings and many other species inhabiting our planet. With an understanding of life's sacred nature comes individual and collective responsibility for nurturing and protecting it.

It is very doubtful that wars could be fought without youth. Generally, older people set wars in motion and call upon younger people to fight them. If enough youth were educated to think for themselves about participating in wars, older people would be forced to find more creative ways to resolve their disputes. Without a willing supply of cannon fodder, wars would cease to be. Older generations would soon find any number of good reasons why they themselves could not or should not fight. Thus, if enough young people were educated to think for themselves about fighting, killing and the value of life, we would be well on our way toward a peaceful world.

Ikeda: I have long advocated that education be free from all interference, separated from politics. Education is not for the benefit of the nation-state but for all humanity.

Krieger: Education for a peaceful world would serve all humanity. Everyone must have what my friend Frank Kelly calls "a seat at humanity's table." We would need to find ways to deal with the legitimate grievances of the poor, downtrodden and oppressed.

Children of the Nuclear Age

Ikeda: The SGI peace movement begins with empathy for others who are suffering.

But I should like to return to the background of your peace activities. You were born in 1942, at about the time when nuclear weapons were being developed. You grew up in the United States during the Cold War. If my generation can be called wartime children, yours might be described as Nuclear Age children. During your student days, your protest against the Vietnam War made a pacifist of you.

Krieger: It is reasonable to characterize my generation as children of the Nuclear Age. That is how I think of myself. In the year of my birth, the physicists Enrico Fermi and Leo Szilard created the first artificial sustained fission reaction. Three years later the United States tested the first nuclear weapon. Three weeks after that, nuclear weapons were used at Hiroshima and then Nagasaki. Of course, I was too young, then, to have any firsthand knowledge of or interest in these events, but I now see how they have affected, even shaped, the lives of my generation and the generations that have followed.

Ikeda: How did Vietnam affect your state of mind?

The Vietnam War

Krieger: The war in Vietnam had an enormous impact on me. It was my generation's war. Whereas nuclear issues lurked in the background, the war affected us directly. We were expected to fight poor peasants on the other side of the world. I am proud to have resisted the Vietnam War because it was based on lies and deception. In a less than democratic spirit, the United States actually refused to allow the Vietnamese people to go ahead with already agreed-on elections when it became clear that Ho Chi Minh would win. To gain approval for the war, Lyndon Johnson lied to Congress about the Gulf of Tonkin incident.[2]

Television treated the conflict like a sporting event, daily reporting body counts of dead Americans and Vietnamese and portraying us as winning because we killed more of them than they did us. I was truly disgusted by what our powerful nation was doing to a small peasant country.

Ikeda: While international-relations professionals were debating the pros and cons of the Vietnam War, Arnold Toynbee demonstrated how a professional in the noblest sense should react to it. He said that the mention of Vietnam made him think of the suffering of the children, the aged and the ill in a land converted into one vast battlefield. For this reason, he wished for the speediest possible peace, no matter what ideology might obtain in a reunited Vietnam. To be worthy of being called an intellectual, one should stand on the side of the ordinary people.

Justice and truth are clear. Participation in the peace movement requires working at the grass-roots level and basing all activities on justice and truth for the ordinary people.

Conscientious
Objection to War

Ikeda: Many young American soldiers were sent to Vietnam from supply bases in Japan, especially Okinawa, which is where I began writing one of my life works—*The Human Revolution*—on December 2, 1964. This narrative history of our movement for peace begins with these words: "Nothing is more barbarous than war. Nothing is more cruel."

The first installment of the book appeared in the *Seikyo Shimbun* newspaper in January 1965. The very next month, the bombing of North Vietnam started. At the time, I was determined that something had to be done to halt the sacrifice of young Americans and of my fellow Asians. In 1966 and 1967, I proposed a cease-fire, a peace conference among the conflicting parties and an end to the bombing of North Vietnam. I directed these proposals especially to young people. In addition, in 1973, I appealed to President Nixon to call for an end to the war.

I understand that because of Vietnam you became a conscientious objector.

Krieger: Yes. In 1964, when I was twenty-two, I returned to the United States after spending nearly a year in Japan. I found I had been drafted into the army and therefore could not join the Peace Corps as had been my plan. I ended up in the army reserves. In 1968, I was called to active duty and assigned to the 442nd Infantry Brigade, which, during World War II, had been a highly decorated unit of Japanese Americans. Before being activated, I was a graduate student at the University of Hawaii, where I had protested against the war.

Ikeda: What was military life like for you?

Krieger: I suddenly found myself a second lieutenant and part of the military machine. But my new position only made me a more active protester. I opposed the war with all my being and knew I would never take part in it. I was resolved not to kill or be killed for a war I did not believe in. This resolution was empowering because it made me realize, at an early age, that the choice was mine.

Ikeda: As your experiences bear witness, human beings are strongest when they choose to follow their conscience.

Krieger: Many of my contemporaries realized the same thing. Some became conscientious objectors. Some left the country. The bravest, in my opinion, went to prison. I tried to become a conscientious objector; but since I was already in the military, and especially as an officer, this was difficult to do. Still, from the day I applied to be a conscientious objector, I never carried a weapon again.

Ikeda: How did the military authorities react?

Krieger: They refused to grant me conscientious-objector status, and I ended up suing them in federal court on a writ of habeas corpus. My contention was that the military was detaining me when I had the right to be free. The army fought hard to keep me in. If they had prevailed, they probably would have court-martialed me for refusing to go to Vietnam. That would have put me in a difficult position. I did not want to go to prison but would have preferred it to going to Vietnam. The problem was resolved without a court-martial because my reserve unit was deactivated and I was honorably discharged. I believe that my actions were honorable.

Family Responses

Ikeda: Your experiences are quite edifying. We sometimes stir up trouble by acting according to our principles. Being prepared for difficulties only reinforces those convictions.

Incidentally, I learned from your wife that she was born in Hawaii five weeks after the bombing of Hiroshima. I sensed the strong will behind her cheerful disposition, and I understand she supported you during your struggle against military service.

Krieger: She stood by me during my time in the military and was a great source of support. We joined the resistance and worked together against the war. Though young herself, she became a draft counselor, advising young men about options such as becoming conscientious objectors.

Ikeda: How did your parents react to your refusal to serve?

Krieger: My mother and father supported me, as did many of my friends. I did not feel alone.

But many others thought I was being disloyal to my country

by challenging the army and refusing to fight. My wife's parents and many of their friends felt that way. They were of the World War II generation and felt strongly about fighting for one's country. Because they did not like what I was doing, our relations with them were strained during that period. Much later they concluded that we had been right about the Vietnam War. But what counted most was not their opinion. We learned the importance of deciding for ourselves what is right and wrong for us. I learned that I had a choice.

Ikeda: Your experiences with your in-laws remind me of a point in Buddhism. Nichiren wrote, "In general, it is the son's duty to obey his parents, yet on the path to Buddhahood, not following one's parents may ultimately bring them good fortune."[1] In other words, temporarily ignoring your parents' instructions in the name of something you know to be absolutely correct benefits parents on a deeper level.

Krieger: I could have gone along with the system by doing what was expected of me, but I chose instead to do what I thought was right. I am very glad I did. In questions of life and death, no one should entrust the decision to another person or to one's government. Nor should one be swayed by public opinion. It is up to individuals to decide for themselves on the basis of conscience.

Ikeda: You illustrate something Tolstoy said about the way to peace: "The time for arguing about the evil of war has passed. The only thing remaining now is for each person to decide where to begin. In other words, each person must refrain from doing things he knows he ought not to do."[2]

Krieger: I hope to teach young people the lesson I learned so that they can avoid the struggle I experienced. If enough young people learn the lesson, we can do away with wars.

Dialogue — A Key to Peace

Krieger: As you learned from Josei Toda, dialogue is basic to understanding different civilizations. My own life experience has made me a firm believer in its importance.

One of the most formative and important experiences of my life was the two years I spent at the Center for the Study of Democratic Institutions, founded by Robert Hutchins. A leading thinker of the mid-twentieth century, Hutchins, at twenty-seven, was dean of the Yale Law School and became, at thirty, president of the University of Chicago.

The Center for the Study of Democratic Institutions, the founding of which was his last great effort, was dedicated to dialogue. It sought to identify and shed light on the most critical matters of the time. Two or three times a week, someone would lead a dialogue on an important issue. Then the other fellows of the Center would discuss the topic in depth in the hope of understanding it better and of developing proposals for the social good.

Ikeda: A fascinating approach. The purpose of dialogue is to delve deeper, understand better and thereby arrive at profound solutions.

Krieger: My desire to join the Center arose from a sense of frustration. In 1972, as a young professor at San Francisco State University, I wanted to see society change. I sought an end to the Vietnam War in particular and to war in general. I promoted firmer adherence to international law and the strengthening of international institutions. But academia seemed too self-contained and surprisingly conventional to offer much hope for such change. In this frame of mind, I attended a symposium sponsored in San Francisco by the Center for the Study of Democratic Institutions.

Ikeda: Academia tends toward isolationism and conservatism. It is necessary instead for institutions of higher learning to reaffirm the principle of serving the people and open themselves to refreshing influences from the community and society as a whole.

A Woman of Vision

Krieger: One of the many symposium speakers captured my interest with her powerful ideas—Elisabeth Mann Borgese, a senior fellow at the Center. In a remarkable talk on creating a new law of the sea and using it as a model for a new world order, she described how powerful modern technologies make possible over-fishing and marine pollution. She also described the great promise that the mineral resources of the ocean floor hold for humanity. She argued that the oceans are our common heritage and that protecting them and managing their resources require a strengthened global order. She believed that, just as life emerged from the seas, so a new world order could emerge from creating a new law for the seas.

The logic and grandeur of her vision excited me. At a more basic level, I was impressed by the very fact of her being a passionate advocate for her vision, a trait I found largely absent in academia. She had recognized a serious problem of enormous proportions and had developed a plan to deal with it and change the world in the process.

After reflecting at home on the symposium, I decided to write to Elisabeth about the possibility of working together.

She responded by inviting me to meet her at the Center for the Study of Democratic Institutions in Santa Barbara. Following that meeting, she offered me a position. That July, my family and I moved to Santa Barbara, where I started the great experience of working with Elisabeth for the next two years.

The power of vision was the most important lesson she taught me. From her, I learned that thinking about creating a better world and working for that end are not crazy. I learned that nearly all of our new technologies are dual-purpose, having potential for both good and evil. The impossibility of containing the effects of new technologies within national boundaries makes new forms of global order necessary.

Ikeda: Vision is the first condition of leadership. Without it, we cannot succeed in the twenty-first century.

Furthermore, the quest to advance technology requires a corresponding spiritual quest. Buddhism always recognizes both aspects of any situation. From this viewpoint, evil and good are seen as two aspects of the same thing. The inner power of human beings determines which aspect will prevail.

Krieger: It is up to the people to choose which technologies should be developed and how to use them.

Ikeda: What kind of a person was Elisabeth Mann Borgese?

Krieger: She was creative and very committed. The daughter of the great German writer Thomas Mann, she studied to be a concert pianist. Just after World War II, she, her husband—a professor at the University of Chicago—and some of their colleagues worked on the Committee to Frame a Constitution for the World. Elisabeth played a major part in writing this great document. I especially like the vision and poetry of its preamble:

"The people of the earth having agreed
that the advancement of man
in spiritual excellence and physical welfare
is the common goal of mankind;
that universal peace is the prerequisite
for the pursuit of that goal;
that justice in turn is the prerequisite of peace,
and peace and justice stand or fall together;
that iniquity and war inseparably spring
from the competitive anarchy of the national states;
that therefore the age of nations must end,
and the era of humanity begin;
the governments of the nations have decided
to order their separate sovereignties
in one government of justice,
to which they surrender their arms;
and to establish, as they do establish,
this Constitution
as the covenant and fundamental law
of the Federal Republic of the World."³

Elisabeth had a strong influence on me, as did the Center itself. But not all the lessons I learned there were positive. I felt the Center was too cerebral and insufficiently action-oriented. Merely talking about change is not enough. It demands action.

Ikeda: "The age of nations must end, and the era of humanity begin." This line especially moves me. It strikes me as a clear vision for the twenty-first century.

Krieger: This is our challenge — to create a new era of humanity by our actions.

Castles in the Sand

Ikeda: As you say, action is crucial. Without it, the noblest ideals are mere castles in the sand.

Krieger: Absolutely. At the Center, however, the fellows were constantly bickering. They could not join in support of common goals. They wasted too much valuable effort jockeying for position. Ultimately, the Center failed to survive its founder for long.

Nonetheless, working with Elisabeth gave me courage and expanded my vision. I greatly respected her and her perseverance in pursuing the goal of a new world order for and from the oceans. In early 2002, I received the sad news of her death, but her work and vision live on.

Ikeda: Have you had other mentors?

Krieger: I have. Among them, my three co-founders of the Nuclear Age Peace Foundation: Wally Drew, Frank Kelly and Charles Jamison. All three are a generation older than I and were veterans of World War II. Unlike many of their contemporaries, they were willing to join in an effort to rid the world of nuclear weapons, strengthen international law and work for a world without war. Each has exhibited courage and wisdom and has advised and guided me. My debt to them is great.

CHAPTER SEVEN

Hiroshima
and Nagasaki

Ikeda: When you visited the Peace Memorial Museums at Hiroshima and Nagasaki in February 1998, you said that all heads of state, particularly the leaders of the nuclear weapons states, should be obliged to visit them, too. In my numerous proposals and on other occasions, I have advocated the same thing, as have many intellectuals and world leaders.

Together, Hiroshima and Nagasaki should be commemorated eternally as the inspiration for anti-war activities.

Krieger: I view Hiroshima and Nagasaki as places made sacred by the many innocent people who died or were injured in the atomic bombings. The victims had the misfortune to be where the door was opened to a new era — the Nuclear Age — in which our human tools for destruction can overwhelm the human capacity for reason. The bombings of Hiroshima and Nagasaki changed our world in far more dramatic ways than most people seem to realize.

Albert Camus perceived this immediately. Two days after the bombing of Hiroshima, in the French resistance newspaper he edited, he wrote: "Technological civilization has just reached its final degree of savagery. We will have to choose, in the relatively near future, between collective suicide and

the intelligent use of scientific conquests.... Faced with the ter-
rifying perspectives which are opening up to humanity, we
can perceive even better that peace is the only battle worth
waging. It is no longer a prayer, but an order which must rise
up from peoples to their governments—the order to choose
finally between hell and reason."[1]

Camus understood how tenuous the future had become.

Ikeda: A true intellectual, he had struggled against Nazism.

Krieger: The best people of his generation fought for elimination of nuclear weapons. Einstein, Russell, Schweitzer, Pauling,
Rotblat and *Saturday Review* editor and citizen-activist Norman
Cousins were among those who spoke out courageously, as
Camus did; each of them leading the fight for the elimination
of nuclear arms and an end to warfare. Your mentor, Josei
Toda, was also among those farsighted leaders. I believe that
future generations will remember them far more favorably than
they will the politicians and military leaders who supported
the nuclear-arms buildup.

Ikeda: The truly courageous person rejects violence and stands
up for the future and the advantage of all humanity. Armed
might symbolizes human cowardice and spiritual defeat.

Krieger: Some people never understood, in the way Camus
clearly did, the terrible force that had been unleashed on
humanity. In describing the bomb to the American people,
immediately after Hiroshima, President Truman said, "We
thank God that it has come to us, instead of to our enemies;
and we pray that He may guide us to use it in His ways and for
His purposes."[2]

Ikeda: Truman's reference to God sounds like an expression of awe at having laid hands on a weapon no one should possess, but nuclear weapons are the product of evil. It is inconceivable that they could serve the purposes of God.

The Courage To Remember

Krieger: The museum in Hiroshima preserves a record of what happened when the bomb was dropped. The city was reduced to ashes. Human beings were incinerated. The beautiful, lively city of Hiroshima today gives little evidence of that instantaneous infliction of massive killing, suffering and damage. Neither does Nagasaki. But unless their tragedies are remembered, understood and acted upon, these tragedies will undoubtedly be repeated with even more devastating consequences.

Ikeda: We can understand tragedy when we face it squarely. Yet, though we are determined never to forget, remembering demands courage.

Krieger: Visits to the Hiroshima and Nagasaki museums would undoubtedly have a sobering effect on the leaders of nuclear-weapons states and could accelerate progress toward achieving the abolition of nuclear weapons.

Ikeda: Buddhism labels as evil anything that works toward human unhappiness. Supreme among the powers of evil is the devil king of the sixth heaven, who is considered a symbol of power lust.

Leaders who really want to exercise their power for the happiness of ordinary people should pay more attention to their own consciences than to bureaucrats, political-party pundits or security advisors. They are required both to be wise and to cultivate all relations, resources and opportunities that further enhance wisdom. This is why world leaders should visit Hiroshima and Nagasaki.

Lessons of the Atomic Bombings

Ikeda: You've said that you date your pacifist work from the visits you made to Hiroshima and Nagasaki in 1963, when you were only twenty-one. How did those visits change your thinking about nuclear weapons?

Krieger: In school, we Americans were taught that the bombings of Hiroshima and Nagasaki were necessary to win the war. I think most Americans still view the use of nuclear weapons in this way. Until I visited the cities myself, I had not stopped to reflect that the bombings were basically attacks against civilian populations. Even today when we in the United States discuss the bombings, the people of Hiroshima and Nagasaki are rarely considered. The lesson in American schools was simplistic: We bombed these two cities and the war ended, therefore the bomb was a good thing. I suspect this interpretation helped make possible the vigorous nuclear arms race during the Cold War.

After visiting Hiroshima and Nagasaki, I came to see that the real lesson was not so simple. Those bombs fell on mostly innocent people. They indiscriminately killed men, women and children, civilians and soldiers. Photographs of the bombed cities, the wreckage and the charred corpses affected me profoundly. I became convinced that, instead of being weapons in some reasonable sense of the word, the atomic bombs were, as the Swedish Nobel laureate and physicist Hannes Alfvén called them, annihilators. My visits to Hiroshima and Nagasaki left me with the desire to play a part in ridding the world of these terrible instruments of destruction.

Ikeda: I understand the shock you felt. No matter how often one goes there, the museums at Hiroshima and Nagasaki always evoke anger, prayer and resolution. It takes courage to face the results of mistakes made by one's own country. I suspect that the people who claim the use of the bombs was unavoidable are actually, if only unconsciously, denying the too-horrible truth. Just as the Germans must face the facts of the Holocaust, and the Japanese the facts of Pearl Harbor, the Nanking Massacre, and the tyrannical invasion of Asia, so are the Americans required to confront their responsibility for Hiroshima and Nagasaki.

But the fate of the two cities has more to teach than pain and remorse. Hope can be found in the strength with which the people restored their cities.

Hope and the Human Spirit

Krieger: The human spirit is remarkable. It has the power to recover from even the greatest tragedy. It can discover hope in places where logic tells us there is none. A flower rising from the ashes of destruction symbolizes it best. If delicate flowers can bud and blossom from the ruins of Hiroshima and Nagasaki, we human beings, too, can rise from such destruction and tragedy.

Ikeda: Your words remind me of Norman Cousins, whom you mentioned earlier and who told me his own visit to Hiroshima had been the turning point in his pacifist work. As a reporter in 1949, when the horrors of the catastrophe were still fresh, he wondered why anyone would return to that scene of immense suffering. He found the explanation in the faces of people on the streets and in the carefree smiles of little children. They taught him that hope and determination to survive are stronger than any devices of war.

This is something for all to remember. Some of my many friends in Hiroshima and Nagasaki lost their entire families in the bombing. Some still suffer aftereffects. Yet, all of them testify to the greatness we human beings can attain.

Krieger: Hiroshima and Nagasaki survivors found the courage and strength to go on living despite the devastation they experienced, including the loss of spouses, parents and children. Knowing of their strength of spirit fortifies my own spirit.

Ikeda: The nuclear abolition movement begins with faith in this internally generated human strength. As a Buddhist, I am resolved to avoid ideological and religious factionalism and to make the well-being of humanity the beginning and end of all actions.

Krieger: I admire this resolve, which I also find in the spirit of my friend Miyoko Matsubara, who was a schoolgirl in Hiroshima when the bomb was dropped. She is committed to working for the elimination of nuclear weapons and to conveying the spirit of Hiroshima. She mastered English so she could tell her story to young people in other parts of the world. I admire her courage and convictions.

Her story, like that of other *hibakusha*—survivors of the bombings— is extremely important. One of its central themes is forgiveness. Having forgiven the United States, she and other *hibakusha* concentrate their efforts on making sure that what happened to them will never happen to anyone else.

I have written some poems about Hiroshima and the *hibakusha*. Here is one about Miyoko:

The Deep Bow of a *Hibakusha*
　for Miyoko Matsubara

She bowed deeply. She bowed deeper than the oceans. She bowed from the top of Mount Fuji to the bottom of the ocean. She bowed so deeply and so often that the winds blew hard.

The winds blew her whispered apologies and prayers across all the continents. But the winds whistled too loudly and made it impossible to hear her apologies and prayers. The winds made the oceans crazy. The water in the oceans rose up in a wild molecular dance. The oceans threw themselves against the continents. The people were frightened. They ran screaming from the shores. They feared the white water and the whistling wind. They huddled together in dark places. They strained to hear the words in the wind.

In some places there were some people who thought they heard an apology. In other places there were people who thought they heard a prayer.

She bowed deeply. She bowed more deeply than anyone should bow.

Ikeda: A moving poem.

I believe it was thirty-five years between your first and second visits to Hiroshima.

Krieger: Yes, and thirty-five years is a long time. Today, the only reminders of the atomic bombing are things that have deliberately been preserved like the famous dome, some monuments and the museum itself. Otherwise, Hiroshima is a bustling and beautiful city where there is a hopeful spirit of rebirth. I am glad a few reminders have been preserved. They remain as warning markers for humanity and also as signs of hope that humanity can triumph over evil. Remembering the Hiroshima and Nagasaki bombings is vital for the future of humanity.

CHAPTER EIGHT

The Season
of Hiroshima

Ikeda: August 6, the day of the Hiroshima bombing, is a special time for the people of Japan to reexamine the issue of peace.

Krieger: Unfortunately, the people of the United States are not as reflective about the events of August 1945 as are the people of Japan. I think of the period from mid-July through mid-August as the season of Hiroshima. It is a time for reflection and contemplation on our responsibilities as human beings to end the nuclear-weapons threat to all life.

Ikeda: When I think about August, I realize all the more fully that Japan and the United States have a special responsibility to fulfill humanity's earnest wish to abolish nuclear weapons. Of course, the United States was the first to develop and use nuclear weapons and, as the sole surviving superpower, is still at the forefront of nuclear technology. Other nations would find it difficult to persist in maintaining such weaponry if the United States decided to renounce it.

Krieger: I agree that the United States and Japan have special responsibilities in seeking to eliminate nuclear weapons. Unfortunately, neither country has really accepted its responsibility.

Ikeda: Perhaps humanity missed the perfect chance to do away with nuclear weapons. Although many years have already passed since 1989 and the exciting end of the Cold War, those arms remain. History now awaits the time when America will fulfill its responsibility to humanity. But actually the American people demonstrate little interest in the nuclear issue. During the Cold War, fear of conflict with the Soviet Union propelled the American nuclear abolition movement. Since then, the people have found no similar fear to serve as a driving force, even though the dangers of nuclear terrorism loom large. It remains to be seen how this situation may change in the aftermath of September 11, 2001.

A certain public-opinion poll showed that, although nearly 90 percent of all Americans approve the idea of an international treaty banning nuclear weapons, practically none express willingness to take action for its sake. The same trend is evident in Japan.

Krieger: You are right to say that American citizens are not focused on nuclear issues. In fact, for the most part, Americans believe the nuclear threat ended with the Cold War. Clearly they are wrong. The nuclear weapons threat remains real and, in some ways, has increased with the breakup of the Soviet Union. The questionable state of controls of the nuclear weapons and weapons-grade materials there should be a wake up call to us all.

Breaking the Silence

Ikeda: In addition to the problem of nuclear control, we are now confronted with proliferation. Indian and Pakistani nuclear tests have awakened the world to the continuing danger of nuclear weapons. In 1990, the two countries were on the brink of nuclear war in a situation Seymour Hersh of *The New Yorker* magazine described as the tensest since the Cuban missile crisis. Recently, they have come to this brink again.

Krieger: It is unclear whether controls in former Soviet Union countries are adequate to prevent weapons and weapons-grade materials from falling into the hands of terrorists, criminals or irresponsible national leaders. After September 11, 2001, we should be acutely aware of our vulnerability to nuclear terrorism. The world has reached a crossroads where either we eliminate nuclear weapons or they will proliferate to many other states and possibly to terrorists as well.

Ikeda: We need those who have heretofore advocated nuclear deterrence to now earnestly consider the risk of continuing with the current non-proliferation regime, with all its weaknesses, versus the risk of putting in place a non-nuclear system. Clearly, without effort toward nuclear abolition, the current non-proliferation regime will sooner or later reach an impasse.

Krieger: How to awaken the American people to the seriousness of the situation is a continuing challenge for our Foundation and for others in the United States. In an article I wrote, "We Are All Culpable,"[1] I argued that a country basing its national security on nuclear weapons, in effect, is basing its security on threatening to murder millions, perhaps hundreds of millions, of innocent people. This is a morally untenable position. Indeed it is less tenable than the position of the German people during the Nazi era. Questioning or criticizing the Nazi government could have resulted in torture or death not only for the questioner but also for his or her whole family. No comparable situation exists in the United States or other Western nuclear-weapons nations. We are free to question the policies of our governments on this issue; nevertheless, there is little protest against nuclear policies. Therefore, if nuclear weapons are used in the future, we will all be culpable. We have the chance to make our voices heard, but most of us fail to speak out. It is a sad commentary on our public morality, which of course reflects our personal morality.

Ikeda: Your efforts at public education are extremely important in this connection. But encouraging efforts are being made on other fronts as well. The New Agenda countries and the non-governmental organization that supports them—the Middle Powers Initiative—are doing important work. I believe you are a member of the Middle Powers Initiative.

As you know, in 1996, retired General Lee Butler, former commander of the U.S. Strategic Command, together with military leaders from many countries, began advocating the abolition of nuclear weapons. On the basis of his own experiences, he explains the danger of accidental detonation and the inefficiency of arms races. Others who have exercised supreme on-site responsibility in nuclear strategy—former U.S. Secretary of Defense Robert S. McNamara and retired Air Force General Charles Horner, who commanded U.S. and Allied air operations during the Persian Gulf War in 1991—have also spoken out. Because of the positions these people occupied, their voices of conscience raised in refutation of the nuclear deterrence concept have tremendous weight and strengthen the worldwide nuclear-abolition movement.

The Rightful Interests of Humanity

Krieger: General Butler was part of the U.S. nuclear weapons establishment. As commander-in-chief of the U.S. Strategic Command, he was in charge of all strategic nuclear weapons.

He was responsible for targeting, and in fact many targets were removed from the U.S. list on his orders. After retiring from the military in 1994, he questioned why more progress toward disarmament had not been made since the end of the Cold War. He became a vigorous advocate of nuclear weapons abolition.

I first met General Butler in 1996 at the State of the World Forum. It is interesting that, although our lives followed very different paths, we ended up at the same place—opposing nuclear weapons. I agree strongly with General Butler's conclusion: "We cannot at once keep sacred the miracle of existence and hold sacrosanct the capacity to destroy it. We cannot hold hostage to sovereign gridlock the keys to final deliverance from the nuclear nightmare. We cannot withhold the resources essential to break its grip, to reduce its dangers. We cannot sit in silent acquiescence to the faded homilies of the nuclear priesthood. It is time to reassert the primacy of individual conscience, the voice of reason, and the rightful interests of humanity."[2]

Ikeda: His very moving conclusion shows immense respect for the dignity of life.

Krieger: General Butler and other members of the Canberra Commission on the Elimination of Nuclear Weapons concluded: "The proposition that nuclear weapons can be retained in perpetuity and never used—accidentally or by decision—defies credibility. The only complete defense is the elimination of nuclear weapons and assurance that they will never be produced again."[3]

Ikeda: The report of the Canberra Commission is epoch-making because of the concrete nuclear abolition process it indicates. Opinions are divided, however, about the methods involved

—for instance, retaining technology to produce nuclear weapons after the weapons themselves have been dismantled (so-called latent deterrence). I believe you and I agree that the goal of their elimination must be the eradication of the will to possess those weapons. From the viewpoint of the dignity of life, that will itself is an ethical violation.

Of course, goals vary. It is necessary for nations to reduce the risk of nuclear weapons gradually by renouncing the use of preemptive strikes and by removing nuclear materials from warheads.

The People Must Awaken

Krieger: One of the great problems we face today is the perception that issues related to nuclear weapons are too complicated for average people, who therefore willingly defer to governments in connection with them.

Ikeda: That is the heart of the issue. General Butler calls the perceived complexity you mention the "nuclear puzzle."

Krieger: Governments of nuclear weapons states have been unwilling to take bold steps toward ending the nuclear weapons era. This situation will alter only if the citizens of those states demand changes from their governments.

It is necessary for the people of the United States and the other nuclear-weapons states to awaken to the dangers that nuclear weapons pose to them and their families as well as to all humanity.

The U.S. government claims to be making progress toward nuclear disarmament. In fact, it has only taken steps to ensure that the status quo of nuclear "haves" and "have-nots" will be maintained for the indefinite future. India repeatedly complained about this arrogant attitude of the nuclear weapons states, and finally India developed its own nuclear weapons capabilities.

Ikeda: And because of the mindset you just explained, criticisms by nuclear nations of the nuclear tests in India and Pakistan are unconvincing.

Krieger: Their criticisms have a hollow and hypocritical ring. In my view, most Americans are asleep on nuclear issues. If they are not awakened, the nightmare will once again become a reality. Of course, the destruction of more cities would wake up Americans and everyone else, too. The challenge is to awaken the public before another disaster occurs. General Butler has tried to do this and so have many other nuclear-abolitionists throughout the world.

Ikeda: The SGI peace movement concentrates on just this kind of awakening and opening of the public's eyes. Some of its focal points are the exhibit "Nuclear Arms: Threat to Our World," anti-war publications, the compiling of signatory petitions, symposia and projects carried out in cooperation with the United Nations.

Why Voices From Hiroshima and Nagasaki Are Not Heard

Ikeda: As the only nation in the world to have suffered nuclear attack, Japan ought to lead the world nuclear abolition movement. But, lacking clear vision, the Japanese government continues to demonstrate a noncommittal, vague attitude toward nuclear abolition.

In fact, lack of official resoluteness is largely responsible for the voices of Japanese atomic-bomb victims failing to affect nuclear nations.

Krieger: Due in part to U.S. government pressure, the Japanese government has not kept faith with its people on the issue of abolishing nuclear weapons. I doubt that any other people oppose nuclear weaponry as fiercely as the Japanese rightly do, knowing firsthand the terrible consequences of nuclear weapons. Hiroshima and Nagasaki survivors know it more clearly than anyone. The *hibakusha* are the true ambassadors of the Nuclear Age.

Ikeda: The government gives short shrift to public opinion on this matter. For example, the World Court delivered the epoch-making decision that using or threatening to use nuclear weapons violates international law. The mayors of Hiroshima and Nagasaki concurred and delivered powerful statements deploring the inhumanity of such weapons. The court was deeply moved. The Japanese government representative, however, made no clear pronouncement on the issue and took pains to disassociate the official government opinion from the two mayors' statements.

In 1994, when the UN General Assembly voted to request an advisory opinion from the International Court of Justice on this matter, the Japanese government representative abstained.

Krieger: On the issue of nuclear weapons abolition, it is impossible for the Japanese government to be true both to the Japanese people and to the U.S. government. The Japanese government seems to believe that the American nuclear umbrella enhances Japanese security, when in fact, it makes the Japanese people accomplices in threats to destroy whole cities, as Hiroshima and Nagasaki were destroyed.

The mayors of Hiroshima and Nagasaki have made many eloquent pleas for the elimination of all nuclear weapons from earth. The government of Japan, however, has shut its ears to these pleas and has gone on playing the role of younger brother to the United States.

In my view, the Japanese government's position is unacceptable; and it is up to the people of Japan to demand that their government's policies conform to the popular will. If they demand this and succeed in changing official Japanese nuclear policies, they could exert a powerful effect on U.S. policies as well. I hope the people of Japan will take the lead in making these demands because it might inspire Americans to demand changes from their government, too.

Ikeda: Johan Galtung, the father of peace studies, is irritated by Japan's failure to make constructive use of its experiences as the only nation to suffer atomic attack. As he said: "Japan should divest itself of its present client status in relation to the United States, thus setting a model of non-aggressive autonomy. Japan could become a first-rate peacemaker, emulating and far surpassing neutral Switzerland."[4] The end of the Cold War gave Japan a chance to demonstrate leadership in the name of peace.

Krieger: I agree with Galtung. It is crucial that Japan assert its independence from U.S. policy. In the post–Cold War world, Japan has a wonderful opportunity to become a much more innovative and assertive leader for peace and a world free of nuclear arms.

Apology: Accepting Responsibility for Past Wrongs

Ikeda: To assume initiative for nuclear weapons abolition, however, entails Japan taking clear responsibility for the war in

Asia, through sincere words and actions free from the taint of diplomatic strategy or equivocation. Unfortunately, other Asian peoples generally interpret the attacks on Hiroshima and Nagasaki as deserved retribution for Japanese invasion and gratefully consider nuclear weapons as having brought the war to an end. Japan's inability to atone for the past casts so long a shadow that voices from Hiroshima and Nagasaki fall on deaf ears. This all means it will take longer to convince other Asian peoples of the threat of nuclear weapons and put them on the path to nuclear abolition. I cannot overstress the importance of this issue.

Krieger: Yes, it is time for Japan's unambiguous apology for past atrocities. I've often wondered why it is so hard for national leaders to apologize for their nations' past wrongdoings. Something in the human psyche seems to inspire belief in one's own group as decent and honorable, even finding ways to justify atrocities. That distorted perception is the rationale for most wars.

Political leaders devise ways to justify even acts of deplorable violence as decent and honorable. But, from even a slight distance, it is clear that many countries behave with considerable indecency and dishonor. In the United States, this has been true in numerous instances, including the genocide of Native American peoples, the crime of slavery, and the war in Vietnam, which many, including myself, feel was carried out illegally.

It costs very little to apologize. Apology clears the air. It demonstrates knowledge of right and wrong and suggests unwillingness to repeat past wrongs. I believe that apologizing benefits the giver more than the recipient. It is a way of lifting a burden and clearing one's soul. In the case of a country, it is a way of clearing the collective soul of the people for past wrongs inflicted in their name. The victim, of course, can forgive the wrong done, with or without an apology.

Ikeda: Your words penetrate to the core of the matter. When based on accurate historical understanding, apology not only atones for the past, it prompts reexamination and contributes to the creation of the future. But confronting mistakes is instinctively repugnant to individuals and to nations as well. True leaders, then, are those who embody a philosophy that enables them to overcome this emotional objection.

Citizens Can Apologize

Krieger: Sometimes, a wronged party forgives even before an apology is made. This is the case with many of the survivors I met in Hiroshima and Nagasaki. Even though the American government has not apologized, the *hibakusha* have forgiven those who dropped the atomic bombs on them.

Apologizing to the Asian peoples who suffered at Japanese hands during the 1930s and 1940s would be an act of catharsis for Japan. It would help Japan redefine itself as a peacemaker in Asia and the world. Apologizing for wrongdoings takes courage. Often politicians are not courageous. If political leaders are unwilling to offer apologies, the next best thing is to offer them person to person, citizen to citizen, as a form of international citizen diplomacy.

Ikeda: You are right. As a Japanese citizen, I have apologized sincerely to the Koreans, the Chinese and other peoples throughout Asia for atrocities committed by Japan. This has been the premise on which my work in culture, education and peaceful exchange in Asia has been carried out. As a Far Eastern island country, Japan has historically received cultural imports from all these peoples. I sincerely feel the need for us to return something to our cultural benefactors.

Krieger: In Hiroshima and Nagasaki, when I have given talks, I have taken the opportunity to apologize, personally as an American, to the audiences I have addressed. I felt it was right for me, as an American, to apologize for the horrible sufferings the bombs inflicted on the citizens of those cities. I hope that someday American political leaders will have the courage to apologize for the suffering we have caused others in the past. The ability and willingness to do so will be a more convincing indication of American greatness than any military force we can mobilize, any weapons we can deploy and any wealth we can accumulate.

Ikeda: True friendship is impossible as long as we shake hands with one hand while holding a weapon in the other. The spirit is cheered not by quarreling but by reconciliation. No one likes a person who refuses to apologize for mistakes. The same is true of nation-to-nation relations. This is a clear and simple truth.

Might and money alone do not make a nation great. A truly great nation—one that deserves respect—is one that cherishes values of the heart and mind.

PART THREE

TRANSCENDING THE NUCLEAR AGE

CHAPTER NINE

The Mission
of Science

Ikeda: Ironically, war has often stimulated scientific and technological development. It has generated much of our current peaceful technology and its byproducts. Similarly, application in warfare has improved much technology originally developed for peaceful purposes.

Krieger: But, of course, this is not an argument for war. Generous funding and the employment of top scientists explain why scientific and technological achievements have resulted from military research. Military establishments, even in peacetime, support the work of a large number of scientists and engineers. I understand that at the height of the Cold War more than half of all nuclear physicists were engaged in military projects. This is a staggering figure. It means that military establishments, to give their projects first priority, largely co-opted scientists and technologists. Thus, the benefits that flow to humanity from research motivated by warfare are really only a cover for the continued use of society's scientific and technological resources primarily for destructive ends. This is a very poor allocation of a society's resources—scientific, technological and financial.

Ikeda: Nuclear power plants are an application of technology developed for nuclear weapons. Though they are usually called peaceful applications, some nuclear reactors actually produce weapons-grade plutonium. As you say, the benefits only cover up destructive aims. Can we do away with these concealed aims? War is the purpose of military technology. If we make war meaningless, can we not rechannel military technology toward peaceful purposes? To do so requires a broad consensus supporting the absolute prevention of war. It also requires us to elevate the lowest common denominator of human morality. Ultimately such achievements would demand organized security among nations and individual human inner reformation.

This is the line of thought behind our continual SGI proposals for UN reform as well as the advancement of a popular world movement founded on peace, culture and education.

When the idea of abandoning war becomes firmly established all over the globe, the peaceful use of technology will become an essential goal rather than a cover.

Krieger: In healthy societies, scientists and technologists would be employed for constructive purposes. Far greater benefits would accrue to humanity from science and technology.

From Club to Nuclear Weapons

Ikeda: In the opening sequence of the movie 2001, *A Space Odyssey,* a man-ape picks up a large bone and swings it first up and then down to crush a skull on the ground. The man-ape then hurls the bone skyward, where it turns end over end. The film then cuts quickly to a spaceship. This juxtaposition of prehistory and the year 2001 symbolizes the millions of years it took for humanity to progress from the origin of tools to space technology.

The man-ape's bludgeon is obviously a weapon not only for killing prey but also for fighting other man-apes. One cannot help wondering how many human lives the progression from club to spaceship has cost. We have moved from club to sword, to pistol, to cannon, to machine gun and finally to nuclear weapons.

Krieger: Throughout history, one of humankind's most pronounced characteristics has been the ability to develop tools. Between the man-ape's weapon and nuclear weapons, efficiency of killing has increased enormously. If our goal has been to improve technologies for destroying one another, we have succeeded dramatically. Scientific discovery and technological achievements have aided us so greatly in this ostensible success that all humanity is now in danger of annihilation. Clearly it is time to re-examine our goals and to cease using science and technology to threaten humanity's very existence.

Ikeda: Though essentially a servant of human happiness, scientific technology now threatens the existence of our whole species.

Reason is unique to humankind. If we employ reason to jeopardize our existence, we are no better than lemmings hurling themselves into the sea. Whether we can live up to our name, *Homo sapiens* — or "thinking humans" — depends on whether we avert this crisis.

Krieger: Science and technology have greatly altered warfare in terms of proximity. It is now possible to kill at greater and greater distances. As a side effect, this has largely deprived warfare of its courageous aspect. What courage is involved in pressing a button to send guided missiles toward targets far out of sight? The ultimate cowardice in war is the threat or use of nuclear weapons. But this cowardice is not attributable solely or even primarily to the military. It is more a cowardice of political leaders, which permeates and spiritually pollutes whole societies. Hand-to-hand combat at least makes killing real without sanitizing it by distance and high-technology instruments of death.

Science and Human Intentions

Ikeda: Even though much scientific technology was developed in connection with military aims, I am by no means anti-science. Clearly science ought to contribute to society's advancement and to improving our standards of living. The point is to reduce the harm and increase the benefit scientific technology proffers; in other words, to find ways of ensuring that technology contributes to human happiness and prosperity.

Science seeks to discover natural and cosmic laws; technology applies the results of scientific research. Whether science and technology are good or bad depend on the goals of the human beings using them.

Krieger: Human intentions play an important role, but it is possible for humans to lose control of their creations.

Ikeda: The Soka Gakkai Okinawa Training Center—which you and your wife visited in February 1998—is located in what was once the base for the Mace B ground-launched cruise missile. The exterior of the former missile-site building is now adorned with statues celebrating life, and the Okinawa SGI youth have installed displays inside that are eloquent testimony to the tragedy of war and the preciousness of peace. The entire center is a monument to world peace and is considered a locus of peace education. Local children and guests from other parts of the country frequently visit. A branch of the Toda Institute for Global Peace and Policy Research will be built on the site. This is one example of a war facility reborn as a transmitter of the message of peace.

As I have said, human beings determine the purposes to which things and technology are put. The strength of one's inner determination will decide whether everything becomes good or bad.

Krieger: Science is a way of understanding nature and the cosmos. I agree that we can use that understanding to benefit humanity and contribute to human happiness, or we can employ it for destructive purposes. The choices are ours and remain available even after the genie has left the bottle.

I was very impressed when I visited the Okinawa Training Center and was happy to see sunflowers growing there from seeds provided by our Foundation.

Every act toward peace is a seed of peace, and each seed has the potential to grow and inspire others. You have provided a useful model in converting a former missile base into a place of peaceful purpose on Okinawa. Something similar has been done in the Ukraine and other parts of the former Soviet Union. Our goal is to continue to plant seeds of peace until all missile bases have been converted to peaceful uses. This requires popular will and determination expressed in political will. Unfortunately, political will in the nuclear-weapons states remains the most important missing element in the global effort to achieve a world free of nuclear weapons.

Science To Benefit Humanity

Ikeda: Under no circumstances, though, can we allow science and technology to be subordinate to nationalist egoism. To prevent this, I have long favored the creation of a conference of scientists as world citizens to represent their nations in discussing how science and technology can be used for the benefit of humankind.

Krieger: All scientists have one qualification of world citizenship: They share scientific methodology as a common language and can often use mathematics to communicate ideas to fellow scientists across linguistic borders. They should know that all humans share a common past and that science has united all humanity in a common destiny. Joining in common purpose, they can help sound once again the alarm bell such great scientists as Einstein, Pauling and Rotblat have sounded in the past.

As you're aware, a conference like the one you suggest was organized in June 2000 by the International Network of Scientists and Engineers for Global Responsibility. Its theme: "The Challenge of Science and Technology in the Twenty-first Century."

Ikeda: At the time, you conducted a sub-conference on eliminating nuclear weapons. What do you feel is the relation among science, technology and peace?

Science, Technology and Peace

Krieger: Science and technology can be used for peace in three important ways. First, technology has a vital role to play in the disarmament process. Technologists can help verify disarmament agreements and develop means of dismantling weaponry. Second, scientists and technologists can work on preventing future conflicts arising from scarcities of such resources as food, water and oil by developing alternatives or through recycling. Third, they can help alleviate current sources of human insecurity related to food shortages, disease and natural disasters. There are many projects to work on, but it is necessary for countries to allocate funds toward these ends just as they now allocate them for military research and development.

Scientists and technologists can be regarded as a societal resource, one that is now devoted too much to destructive instead of constructive ends. On the other hand, scientists and technologists are not inanimate objects but human beings individually responsible for their actions. There is no legitimate reason to contribute one's talents knowingly to any aspect of creating or developing weapons of mass destruction. Doing so is an illegal act under international law — preparation for a crime against humanity or a war crime. Scientists and technologists must be warned and urged never to become parties to such crimes by giving their talents to the creation, development, testing, maintenance or use of such terrible weapons.

Ethical Principles

Ikeda: Adopting sound ethical principles, they must courageously and staunchly refuse to endorse nation-state logic. Society, in turn, must provide an environment supportive of the conscientious acts of scientists and technologists. We need an organized support system so they will not be isolated. That sort of system, if expanded and widely understood, would be highly influential.

Krieger: While the major purpose of science is to explore and understand the natural world, those are not complete ends; they merely reflect curiosity. Some other propelling force—

benefit to humanity—is necessary. I therefore urge scientists and technologists to reject all governmental requests to do anything detrimental to human benefit—like developing tools of warfare. They should never allow themselves to be used as tools in the development of ever-more-powerful instruments of annihilation.

Ikeda: In Buddhist terminology, unconscionable people who use their abilities solely for personal avarice and fame are called talented beasts. No doubt because he recognized the danger of becoming a talented beast, Hippocrates made high ethical demands of people engaged in medicine. The celebrated Hippocratic Oath requires physicians not to misuse their position or knowledge for personal gain and always to be moderate and restrained in dealings with patients. It is founded on a spirit of service that triumphs over personal greed and egoism. Today, all intellectually trained people—not just scientists and technologists—can learn much from the spirit of the Hippocratic Oath. Indeed, perhaps they should take a similar oath pledging to use their knowledge and skills conscientiously for the welfare and happiness of all humankind. Joseph Rotblat has proposed that fledgling scientists voluntarily take such an oath. A considerable movement is under way among like-minded young people.

Krieger: That is very important. Far from improving the lot of humanity, science without ethics can lead to disaster. Enormous responsibility is involved. Before acquiring specialized knowledge, scientists and technologists should study and develop sound ethical foundations. Unfortunately, far too little consideration is given to ethics in modern institutions of higher education.

Modern Times

Ikeda: Modern technology makes possible things once unthinkable. Human beings have landed on the moon. Information dispersal via the Internet transcends national borders. Average human life spans have increased. But are human beings really happier today than in times gone by?

Human desires are limitless. As soon as one is satisfied, a new one takes its place. The will to gratify our desires has stimulated development and served as the main driving force enabling civilization to flourish. Today, however, it tends to deprive us of independence and inhibit our humanity. Selfish desire—which Buddhism defines as greed—is an impulse that pursues gratification even at the cost of destruction and harm to others.

While fundamental human desire energizes the search for happiness, when transformed by egoism into greed it causes grief for both the self and the other. It can enslave us to techno-scientific civilization as illustrated by Charlie Chaplin's movie *Modern Times.*

Krieger: Modern societies enjoy conveniences that kings of the past would have envied. Still, as you point out, the question remains as to whether our lives are meaningful and fulfilled. This, of course, takes us into the realm of philosophy.

I wonder how many people today grapple with the question of what constitutes a meaningful life. Western societies tend to identify meaningfulness with accumulation. We reward and honor people who most successfully accumulate goods or the money to acquire them. As long as consumerism drives our economies, the ability to accumulate is considered an end in itself. But this superficial formula is a very improbable way to human fulfillment. How can material things—no matter how new or elegant—replace the simple pleasures of friendship, sharing, learning, loving, being creative or appreciating beauty?

Ikeda: When first applied to the cosmos and the material world, the objective search for truth through modern scientific analysis and synthesis proved extremely effective. When applied to the ultimate realms of the physical world and to life and the spirit, however, it demonstrates limitations and exerts an ominous influence.

The elimination of smallpox was a brilliant medical achievement. Cloning, too, is technically brilliant, but it engenders grave ethical problems and dignity-of-life concerns. Everything that is born must die. All things that have life are subject to aging and illness. Curing illness and prolonging life are conducive to human happiness. But unless our value criteria and lifestyles take into consideration the way they are put to use, technologies for achieving these aims can actually invite unhappiness.

Though immortality without aging is an ancient human dream, the repeated use of biotechnology to prolong mere physical life doesn't ensure happiness. In her famous novel, Mary Shelley describes the grief the monster created by Dr. Frankenstein's egoism experiences at his deformed appearance. We can learn much from this.

Krieger: Cloning can trivialize the value of life and remind us that our knowledge exceeds our wisdom. Still, serious thought about it can restore some basic human values and stimulate us to ponder the meaning of life. Questioning new technologies may help us create more decent societies in which individuals are valued for who they are, not what they have.

Wisdom can guide the way we live. Usually simple, it is

often embodied in folk tales and fables or found in the basic principles of the world's great religions.

Ikeda: The scientific worldview stresses quantity of knowledge and rational thought. Most important, however, is whether such knowledge serves human happiness. The flaw in the currently prevailing scientific or utilitarian view is to mistake knowledge for wisdom and to equate increasing knowledge with happiness. Scientific technology invites great peril when its logic pursues its own course.

The wise course is to control and make correct use of knowledge. Buddhism is a means for developing wisdom, and it teaches how to overcome the four inherent sufferings or sorrows—birth, aging, illness and death—in order to lead a happy, meaningful life. In addition it teaches how to control desire rather than be controlled by it.

Krieger: If we can control our desires, we can be happy with life's simple pleasures. Most important, we can live as though life truly mattered. Living is rich if we focus constantly on the miracle that is life.

Knowledge and Wisdom

Ikeda: What do you find wanting in modern—especially scientific-technological—civilization? What philosophy does a person living in that civilization require?

Krieger: Your questions go to the heart of what we are as human beings and what we desire to be. I think what is most wanting is the ability of individuals to think critically and to base their choices and actions on sound ethical foundations. Like you, I am troubled by modern society's confusion of knowledge and wisdom. Knowledge helps us understand the world we live in better but does not necessarily help us determine the best course of action. Wisdom, on the other hand, establishes a direction. It transcends knowledge. It is knowledge tempered by experience and rooted in values. For example, knowledge provides tools for trans-border communications but offers no guidance on what to communicate. It can be used either to exploit or to help others. It can be used to exploit the environment and natural resources for the sake of personal gain or to protect them for future generations. The choice is ours. Knowledge cannot help us make it; wisdom can.

I think a person in modern society should be guided by living simply, contributing to the happiness of others and building a more decent and equitable world.

Ikeda: Hippocrates said that the doctor who loves wisdom is equal to the gods. Guided by wisdom, knowledge can manifest limitless power.

If wisdom is like water, education is like the pump. In the years to come, the role of education in developing and nurturing wisdom will become increasingly vital.

It is important to learn from the wisdom of the past, too. Oral histories and literary and folk traditions often contain abundant wisdom accumulated through long experience. Throughout the process of modernization people have overlooked or undervalued the old and have abandoned things nurtured in tradition. But to break with the wisdom accumulated and distilled over hundreds of generations is a tremendous loss. Listening humbly to the wisdom of our forebears can enrich our modern life.

The Three Cs

Krieger: In the course of a lifetime, most people acquire some wisdom. It is interesting that modern societies give greater emphasis to bequeathing wealth than to transmitting wisdom. Laws provide for passing on property to the next generation, but little thought is given to leaving them wisdom. Although our libraries are filled with knowledge, it is up to each of us to discover the wisdom that will be our guide. Universities are largely purveyors of knowledge. They offer little guidance and few models with regard to wisdom or values.

In such an age, I suggest a philosophy focused on the three Cs: compassion, courage and commitment. A life founded on this philosophy would be one of service not accumulation. It would oppose violence and discover value in others.

Ikeda: Compassion in its deepest form — what we call Buddhist mercy — is the fountainhead of courage and commitment. Your wonderful, humanistic idea of these three Cs accords with the SGI's aims. Indeed, the three Cs are the mainstays of our movement — compassion for our suffering friends, courage to confront evil and commitment to stimulate each individual to act. These are the things that have enabled SGI Buddhists worldwide to acquire wisdom to overcome hardship, to understand and support others and to master oneself, while making perseverance and tolerance our foundation.

Krieger: Inherent in compassion is a belief in human dignity that extends across all borders. Compassion cannot be limited by artificial boundaries. Living a compassionate life requires courage and commitment. Underlying such a philosophy is the belief that individuals can make a difference. I believe this and look to Gandhi, Schweitzer, King, Mother Teresa, Rosa

Parks and Cesar Chavez as examples of lives of compassion, courage and commitment.

Science and Spirituality

Ikeda: As we said earlier, modern science observes and investigates the laws of the physical world. It ensures its observational objectivity through analysis, synthesis and by establishing an oppositional, subject-object relationship. At one end of the scale, scientific method delves into the uncertainties of quantum theory; at the other, it expands to explain the universe as in Einstein's theory of relativity. In addition, modern science investigates genetics, bioengineering and the brain. Psychology and psychiatry have made great forward strides. And in areas like ecology, quantum theory, relativity and psychology, the developments of modern science and Buddhist teachings see eye to eye. Ideas on ecology correspond to the Buddhist teaching of dependent origination,[1] and quantum theory and relativity accord with the Buddhist concept of the oneness of all things.

Krieger: Certainly, human beings need both science (rationality) and spirituality (intuition). The best science is often infused with intuition.

Ikeda: The Buddhist teaching of the nine consciousnesses delves deep into our inner world to reveal the basic self. It first identifies six kinds of consciousness based on the five senses plus the mind. Below them is what is called the *mano*-consciousness. Always active, this level discerns the inner world and is said to be the place where strong attachment to the self is operative. In Western terms, it corresponds to the Freudian subconscious. Below the *mano*-consciousness is the *alaya-*

consciousness, which forms the foundation of the preceding seven consciousnesses. It corresponds to the Jungian collective unconscious. It may be either pure or tainted by karma. One school of philosophy[2] regards this level as the bedrock of the self. Others,[3] however, posit a ninth or *amala*-consciousness, which is completely free of karmic impurity.

Krieger: Although I am not familiar with the nine consciousnesses concept, I am impressed by this detailed analysis of the unconscious formulated long before Freud and Jung.

The Human Revolution

Ikeda: Whereas science begins with a reformation of the external world, Buddhism starts with reforming the inner human world—what we call the *human revolution*—and moves on to society. If we want to halt the excesses of science and technology and save humanity from the crises confronting contemporary civilization, we can no longer merely treat the symptoms.

Krieger: The revolution of the inner world you propose is essential for humanity's future. Indeed, if we go on consuming as we have in the past, we cannot be assured that humanity will have a future at all. As Buddhism insists, control of our desires is critical. This means living more simply and finding satisfaction in ways other than by possessing things. You have suggested transcending egoism and living altruistically as ways to remain in the ninth state of life, the world of Bodhisattva.

Living altruistically means finding satisfaction in doing things for others. Perhaps this is the key to liberation from the dominance of materialism. A person in the grip of materialism wants to know, "What's in this for me?" A person living altruistically asks, "What can I do for you?" The two orientations are very different. The former promotes accumulation and egoism, whereas the latter promotes giving, sharing and loving.

Your concept of altruism is similar to what I mean by compassion. It seems to be compassion in action. Although important, compassion is not enough. It must be put into action.

Ikeda: Nichiren spoke of earthly desires being used as fuel for the flame of wisdom. Buddhism teaches the converting of personal ambitions and desires, even base ones, into good traits like wisdom through altruistic living. A Buddhist doctrine that earthly desires *are* enlightenment indicates that greed, anger (violence) and egocentricism can be transformed into altruistic traits like compassion, trust and nonviolence. The underlying delusions that drive our desires—including the desire for the development of science and civilizations—can be essentially transformed in a way that changes selfishness into altruism, violence into nonviolence and suspicion into trust. Buddhism teaches that the altruistic way of life glows with the flame of wisdom. The bodhisattva way is to let wisdom put knowledge to use and to couple compassion with compassionate action.

Brilliance Is Not Enough

Krieger: How many bodhisattvas will it take to change the world? How much altruism? We cannot answer these questions. We can only say that it will take more of both than currently exist. Education should enable us to increase both the number of bodhisattvas and the amount of altruism. But we need an education different from what is current. Until now, education has concentrated on practical tasks like reading, writing and arithmetic. But this kind of schooling is insufficient to eliminate the severe threats our species faces. We now require education in compassion and altruism; education that places a supreme priority on reverence for life. This kind of education can become the basis for an inner revolution.

Scientists and technologists are often among the most brilliant members of society. They excel in gathering and ordering knowledge. Frequently they are very creative. But science and technology without compassion and altruism have brought us to the brink of disaster. Brilliance is not enough. Mastery of knowledge is insufficient. Creative people must realize what they are creating and understand the consequences.

Ikeda: The founder of Buddhism, Shakyamuni, once severely scolded some brilliant disciples. They had heard many teachings and understood basic principles, and they concentrated exclusively on their own attainment of enlightenment. He told them that just as a split stone cannot be rejoined and parched grain can never germinate, so they would never attain Buddhahood. The reason behind the scolding was this: Although the disciples in question were of superior ability and exerted great influence on others, they performed no altruistic acts and were in danger of cloistering themselves within their own egos. Shakyamuni was attuned to the danger of people who, though intellectually superior, lack compassion.

Krieger: An altruistic world requires us to act with compassion. A peaceful world demands that we act for peace. An equitable world will be created when we live justly. The power of words to stimulate change is far less than the power of actions. Our actions will set an example for those around us. The future we want will be shaped through our daily actions and decisions.

To overcome the crises we now face, we need to change in fundamental ways, to return to our very roots.

Ikeda: In a discussion of environmental issues, Aurelio Peccei, founder of the Club of Rome, told me that overcoming the crises we face requires a revolution of humanity itself. The various and necessary ways of transforming our ego-driven and greed-affirming society will founder without a fundamental inner human revolution.

Krieger: Human beings are thinking and feeling animals. We have the grace of life and share our world with many other creatures. We have the responsibility to pass our world on, intact, to succeeding generations. If we could return to basic ideas like these, if we could slough off all pretensions and return to who we really are, we could live lives filled with happiness that is centered on the simple joys of being, giving and loving.

Ikeda: That is the key to successful coexistence within the limited environment of our planet. True equality means the joy of coexistence with others.

Taking Risks for Humanity

Krieger: Our development as a species has reached the point where it is required that we take some risks for humanity. One such risk is to take a chance on finding better ways than violence to resolve our differences. Another is to risk sharing in the belief that what we do for others will make our own lives richer.

Ikeda: Risky adventures like those are of primary importance. They represent altering our ways of thinking about human life and society and the struggle against selfish desire.

Krieger: Humanity needs a new set of heroes. It is time we toppled from their pedestals figures whose place in history depends on triumphing over others. Instead, let's replace them with the figures of individuals who have found cures for illnesses, who have improved food supplies, who have discovered and implemented nonviolent ways of resolving conflict and who have lived in the spirit of altruism. We can rid ourselves of war and other scourges when we cast violence from our hearts and realize that our dignity depends on the dignity of the other human beings with whom we share this beautiful planet.

Ikeda: The whole world depends on mutual interdependence. Nothing exists in isolation. Modern cosmology, the results of ecological study and the Buddhist doctrine of dependent origination all teach us this: We live in a system of interrelations with other humans, nations, societies and the natural world. Human spiritual poverty spews forth in war and environmental pollution, which disrupt these relations.

CHAPTER TEN

The Challenge of Abolition 2000

Ikeda: According to recent information, some thirty thousand nuclear warheads still exist. Though a reduction below Cold War levels in destructive power, this stockpile represents the equivalent of three hundred thousand bombs of the type dropped on Hiroshima.[1] Given these circumstances, can we assure a nuclear–free future?

There are both dark and light sides to the story. On the dark side are the U.S. Senate's refusal to ratify the Comprehensive Test Ban Treaty[2] and the escalating conflict between India and Pakistan, both of which possess nuclear weapons. On the encouraging side is the rising popular voice in favor of nuclear weapons abolition. This demonstration of will indicates the growing power of nongovernmental organizations, an excellent example of which is the Abolition 2000 network you helped to found.

Krieger: Abolition 2000 embodies the enormous challenge of bringing the voices of people throughout the world to bear on whether to maintain or abolish nuclear weapons. Originating at the 1995 Non-Proliferation Treaty Review and Extension Conference[3], Abolition 2000 took as its goal the conclusion, by the year 2000, of a treaty for the phased elimination of nuclear weapons within a time-bound framework. We thought it was important to enter the twenty-first century with a solid commitment in place. We did not succeed in realizing this goal within the timeframe, but we have not given up.

Abolition 2000 began with only a few groups. But they have grown into a network of more than two thousand organizations and municipalities in more than ninety nations. These groups represent ordinary people's desire to live in a world without threat of nuclear annihilation; they give voice to those who believe in their right to live in such a world. Because there are two thousand groups, it gives new meaning to the name Abolition 2000.

Ikeda: As we have already said, NGOs hold the key to the elimination of nuclear weapons. Obviously, conventional nation-state negotiations cannot solve the problems confronting humankind today.

In existing circumstances, however, though many individual nations operate under some form of democratic system, international society still lacks a way to make the voice of the people accurately heard. The continued existence of nuclear weapons in spite of ordinary people's widespread desire for their abolition bears eloquent witness to this. As the United Nations is still governed by nation-states, the heavy responsibility to represent the popular will in international society falls to nongovernmental organizations.

Krieger: I agree that NGOs have a crucial role in representing and reflecting the voices of ordinary people. NGOs are the counterweight to the corporate interests that have developed such extraordinary influence over democratic governments. Real democracy demands that the voices of the people be heard and that their interests be served. I believe we must never give up the fight to achieve a world free of the threat of nuclear annihilation.

Ikeda: If we don't go on fighting, the path to nuclear-arms abolition may remain inaccessible.

Krieger: The important thing with Abolition 2000 was not so much reaching our goal by the year 2000 as it was educating the world that we must abolish nuclear weapons sooner rather than later or never.

A focal point of such efforts was the Sixth Review Conference of the Nuclear Non-Proliferation Treaty, held in April and May 2000 at the UN Headquarters. This treaty now has participation from 187 countries. We at the Nuclear Age Peace Foundation published opinions on necessary steps in the *The New York Times* on April 24, 2000, the opening day of the conference. They took the form of an "Appeal To End the Nuclear Weapons Threat to Humanity and All Life," which was signed by many global leaders including Jimmy Carter, former U.S. president; Oscar Arias Sánchez, former president of Costa Rica; and Joseph Rotblat of the Pugwash Conferences. You, too, endorsed the Appeal, which stated in part, "The only way to assure that nuclear weapons will not be used again is to abolish them." I presented both this Appeal and an oversized copy of the Abolition 2000 International Petition, which has been signed by some thirteen-and-a-half million people, to Ambassador Abdallah Baali of Algeria, president of the conference.

Looking the Threat in the Face

Ikeda: The conference had an important influence on future advances in nuclear disarmament. Unfortunately, concrete plans for abolition were not forthcoming. Nonetheless, for the first time, nuclear-weapons nations made a clear promise to eliminate their weapons. This was encouraging, although they have done virtually nothing toward fulfilling that promise. Also deserving special notice is the inclusion of other nations besides just the United States and Russia in the nuclear weapons–abolition process.

Krieger: Predictably, the conference witnessed sharp conflicts of opinion between the nuclear "have" and "have-not" nations. For a while, it seemed no final statement would be adopted. Ultimately, however, the parties to the treaty broke through the stalemate and reached consensus. There is still much work to do. Many of the articles prescribe no definite measures or time limits. Responsibility to faithfully implement the consensus rests with the nuclear powers.

How will they go about it? As long as the nuclear-weapons states stick to outmoded policies of deterrence, their clear promise to eliminate those weapons will remain empty.

Ikeda: I agree. With the results of the 2000 Review Conference of the Nuclear Non-Proliferation Treaty, the stage moved to the UN Conference on Disarmament in Geneva as a place for multinational negotiations. But this conference ended without even establishing a working document toward further deliberation. This state of affairs provided cause for great concern. It was not so much the conference system that led to the stalemate as the nuclear states' lack of clear political will to eliminate nuclear weapons. Thanks to the leadership of non-nuclear nations in the New Agenda group and the NGOs supporting them, nuclear weapons nations at the 2000 Review Conference finally recognized a written promise for the total elimination of these weapons. To prevent a reversal of this course, we must reinforce the surrounding net of public opinion. At the same time, it is necessary to press nuclear weapons nations to honor their promises.

Krieger: This is why we are collecting signatures of endorsement to our "Appeal To End the Nuclear Weapons Threat to Humanity and All Life" all around the world.[4]

Ikeda: After long years of negotiations, we have reached a consensus. But this does not mean the nuclear threat has diminished. The arms race continues in different forms. It's like the Greek myth of Sisyphus who was doomed to roll a heavy stone uphill only to have it always roll back down. We must call a halt to this tragedy. On the basis of article six of the Nuclear Non-Proliferation Treaty, it is crucial that we initiate the arms-reduction process immediately and designate the first ten years of this century as the Decade for the Elimination of Nuclear Weapons.

The UN General Meeting of 2000 resolved to set certain important goals like putting the Comprehensive Test Ban Treaty into effect by 2003 and concluding the Fissile Material Cutoff Treaty[5] by 2005. Setting these clear goals to prevent further arms races is important. But it is only a start. It is necessary for us to go further, to do our utmost to encourage the nuclear nations to implement reductions.

The 2000 Review Conference agreed to forming a subcommittee to deal with nuclear arms reduction at the Geneva Conference on Disarmament. The subcommittee, however, should frame a schedule for these reductions and check to see that nuclear weapons nations undertake concrete actions.

Krieger: I agree entirely. The consensus to eliminate nuclear arsenals represents the triumph of the upraised voices of peoples everywhere. We must compel the nuclear nations to implement it faithfully.

To break the snail's pace of reductions bound up in perceptions of national interests requires leaders of the nuclear-weapons states to see those weapons and their reliance upon them for the true threat they pose to humanity.

The longer abolition is postponed, the more likely nuclear weapons will either be used or will proliferate to other countries or to terrorist groups. Obviously, nuclear weapons in terrorist hands would present a profound, perhaps insurmountable challenge to democratic societies.

The World Court Project

Ikeda: The transnational and popular solidarity that NGOs are building really affects national policies. For instance, indicative of its influence, the World Court Project, which cooperated with Abolition 2000, successfully convinced the International Court of Justice to deliver an advisory opinion on nuclear weapons.

Krieger: The World Court Project paralleled Abolition 2000 and involved many of the same organizations and individuals. It was a citizens' movement to bring before the International Court of Justice the illegality of the threat or use of nuclear weapons.

Ikeda: We were all greatly encouraged by the Court's opinion that the threat or use of nuclear weapons violates international law and that all nations are obligated to negotiate sincerely and come up with measures for their elimination.

Krieger: The initiative of the World Court Project was a striking success. Within only a few years, the project got both the World Health Organization and the UN General Assembly to ask the Court for an advisory opinion on the legality of the threat or use of nuclear weapons. On July 8, 1996, the Court issued its historic opinion, about which I have written a book with Ved Nanda, a human rights expert and a distinguished professor of international law at the University of Denver College of Law.

Ikeda: Of course, it wasn't easy to have the nuclear weapons issue brought to the court. Nuclear nations did all they could to thwart the resolution's adoption by the UN General Assembly. Nonetheless, encouraged by a group of NGOs, nations eager for disarmament banded together to get the issue heard.

The ICJ Advisory Opinion

Krieger: The hearing before the Court was quite contentious. The nuclear-weapons states argued for the legality of these weapons under international law. Most other states appearing before the Court, however, argued that nuclear weapons cannot be used without violating the most fundamental principles of international humanitarian law. These principles include distinguishing between combatants and civilians and not using weapons that cause unnecessary suffering.

In the end, the Court called the threat or use of nuclear weapons generally illegal. It could not decide, however, whether the threat or use of nuclear weapons under existing international law would be legal or illegal in extreme circumstances of self-defense, when the very survival of a state was at stake. Partly because of this ambiguity, the Court felt compelled to unanimously assert the obligation to negotiate and conclude a treaty on nuclear disarmament in all its aspects. In other words, the Court essentially adopted the Abolition 2000 position, although not its timeframe.

Ikeda: The Court's advisory opinion should accelerate the pace of abolition action. The month after it was announced, the nonaligned nations presented an action plan to the UN Conference on Disarmament in Geneva. Then the Canberra Commission convened by the Australian government presented its "Report on the Elimination of Nuclear Weapons," setting forth a three-stage scheme for the achievement of the goal.

In September 1996, the UN General Assembly adopted the Comprehensive Test Ban Treaty. The antinuclear appeal that same year, issued by former military leaders from various nations, had tremendous impact. With the signing of the Africa Nuclear Weapons–Free Zone Treaty in April 1996, the entire Southern Hemisphere — including South Africa, which once possessed nuclear armaments — became nuclear-weapons free. I understand that other groups cooperating with Abolition 2000 have compiled a draft for a total abolition treaty.

Krieger: Yes. Some NGOs prepared a draft treaty. It is called the Model Nuclear Weapons Convention. With technical assistance from the International Network of Engineers and Scientists Against Proliferation, the Lawyers Committee on Nuclear Policy coordinated the effort. The document they produced was introduced into the General Assembly by Costa Rica and has been widely circulated among UN delegations. It provides a framework for and demonstrates the technical feasibility of a treaty abolishing nuclear weapons.

Other Approaches to Abolition

Ikeda: Drawing up an abolition process during the fierce Cold War confrontation between the United States and the Soviet Union was difficult. Now, in addition to Abolition 2000, several other organizations have made concrete proposals, like the Canberra Commission Report and the Report of the American Academy of Sciences. Canadian Senator Douglas Roche, the former Canadian ambassador for disarmament, has evolved the idea of a coalition of middle-power nations to address disarmament. You also participate in this work. This coalition concept insists that nuclear powers be unequivocally committed to eliminating nuclear weapons and should take concrete steps at once — going off alert status and vowing to make no preemptive strikes.

Krieger: It is an important approach. The Middle Powers Initiative has sent delegations to key middle-power nations, including many nonnuclear NATO nations. The goal of these delegations has been to influence these governments to put pressure on the nuclear weapons states to take concrete steps toward eliminating their nuclear arsenals. I participated in one such delegation to Japan along with General Butler, Secretary McNamara, retired British Navy Commander Robert Green, Hiro Umebayashi, executive director of the Pacific Campaign for Disarmament Security, and others.

Ikeda: People who claim abolition is unfeasible advance three major obstacles: developing a perfect inspection system, preventing nuclear weapons knowledge and technology from falling into the hands of terrorists or nations on the verge of producing their own weapons, and doing away with the knowledge once it has been acquired. How can we refute these objections?

Krieger: An inspection system can be developed with a combination of technological means and on-site inspections. In a process of phased reductions, confidence will be built with each succeeding phase. Clearly terrorists would have a much more difficult time acquiring nuclear weapons when the number of weapons has been greatly reduced. The know-how to make nuclear weapons will never go away, so we will need effective international controls on all nuclear materials. A good start has been made in this direction, but far stronger controls are needed. No one suggests that eliminating nuclear weapons will be easy, only that it is necessary. The most important missing element is political will. If we had the political will, I believe the other obstacles could be overcome.

Struggling Against Despair

Ikeda: The United States and Russia have agreed on further reductions, and Britain has decided to reduce its weapons and relax its firing stance. Aside from this modest progress, however, nuclear weapons nations demonstrate no sincere effort to implement the International Court of Justice's advisory opinion. Probably, they still cannot break with the outdated nuclear-deterrence idea.

Nuclear testing in India and Pakistan and the U.S. Senate's refusal to ratify the Comprehensive Test Ban Treaty have put nuclear abolition behind schedule. Russia, reacting against NATO's eastward expansion, has overturned the Gorbachev-era pledge to use no preemptive strikes.

Facing a changing international situation, the abolition movement has to battle against despair and giving up. No doubt you have experienced both joy and pain in your work.

Krieger: I believe that with knowledge comes responsibility, and giving up is not an option. The pain I have felt in my work to abolish nuclear weapons is of the kind involved in any struggle to achieve something worthwhile. It is the pain of being rebuffed and of not being taken seriously by people with power to bring about change. I have also felt the pain of realizing what needs to be done but being unable to find the strategy for success.

I suppose we have succeeded to an extent since more and more people now take nuclear-weapons abolition seriously. NGOs once hostile to the very use of the word *abolition* now embrace it in their platforms.

Ironically, as popular support for abolition has grown, governments of nuclear-weapons states have become more intransigent. I have, however, found joy in the struggle to achieve a goal that I know is right. My joy has been in watching the movement grow. It has been in seeing young people join our efforts for a world free of nuclear weapons. It has been in meeting and working with remarkable people throughout the world. It has been in trying to stretch myself to help accomplish what I consider to be the single greatest challenge of our time. My joy has been in sharing my convictions with others, in sowing seeds of peace. The joy of the struggle has far outweighed the pain.

Ikeda: How would you describe the task of Abolition 2000?

Sounding the Alarm

Krieger: It is important to emphasize the nature of Abolition 2000 as a network to which each group brings its own particular focus and skills. The network includes professional groups, such as doctors and lawyers, peace groups, human rights groups, environmental groups, religious groups and many others. As a network, it has both strengths and weaknesses. Among its strengths are diversity and shared responsibility. Lack of a clear organizational structure is a weakness. Thus far, it has lacked the focus and unity of the International Campaign to Ban Landmines. If it succeeds, it will mark a great victory for humanity.

Ikeda: How would you evaluate its significance?

Krieger: It is difficult to evaluate the meaning of any movement. I think Abolition 2000 has placed the bar high. We have changed the terms of the discussion. Before Abolition 2000, there was no active global campaign for abolishing nuclear weapons. Most concerns for nuclear weapons were dealt with by what is termed *arms control*. The position of Abolition 2000 is that arms control is not enough. Even disarmament is not enough. We had to raise the bar to the level of abolition. In a limited sense we have succeeded. Even nuclear-weapons states now realize that the ultimate goal is abolition, though, at their preferred rate, it may not come until the year 3000.

I suppose the significance of the Abolition 2000 movement lies in having helped sound the warning call to humanity. We have helped give notice; we have said clearly that the status quo is not acceptable. We have added our voices to the struggle for human decency and survival.

Ikeda: Based on the Buddhist teaching of the dignity of life, we in the SGI are convinced of and have consistently affirmed innate human goodness. This is why we find it deeply meaningful to cultivate public opinion in favor of nuclear-arms abolition. Nuclear "have" nations obstinately argue that abolition would deprive them of status. The voice of the people argues that the very possession of nuclear weapons degrades a nation's status. We are resolved to help the voice of the people drown out the "have" nations' obstinate insistence.

CHAPTER ELEVEN

The Abyss
of Total Annihilation

Ikeda: Arnold J. Toynbee, whom I've discussed previously, was one of the most outstanding historians of the twentieth century. He once told me that three religions had filled the spiritual vacancy left in the West by the ebbing of Christianity: nationalism, communism and faith in scientific progress.[1] Yet, the initiation of the Nuclear Age in 1945, and World War II itself, made it painfully clear that science does not always work for the good of humanity.

In the nineteenth and twentieth centuries, rapidly increasing knowledge made possible dramatic scientific advances. But knowledge itself lacks the power to bring fundamental salvation. It is not a god.

Humanity in the Nuclear Age, believing too much in the omnipotence of science, has abandoned responsibility for controlling it. From the instant of the first nuclear explosion in the desert near Alamogordo, New Mexico, reevaluating faith in science and restoring human independence of thought and action have become critical to the preservation of our species.

Krieger: In the Nuclear Age, our technologies have become powerful enough to destroy us. This is something new in human history and demands a wise response. But humankind continues as though nothing has changed. Our response to the very real dangers of nuclear annihilation has been far from adequate.

Ikeda: For the first time since the dawn of humanity, we gaze into the abyss of total annihilation. In his memoirs, J. Robert Oppenheimer, once scientific director of the Manhattan Project, said that as he witnessed the first atomic explosion he recalled a passage from the Bhagavad Gita: "If the radiance of a thousand suns were to burst at once into the sky, that would be like the splendor of the Mighty One.... I am become Death, the destroyer of worlds."[2]

Krieger: The challenge of preventing nuclear annihilation deserves our full attention and our best global efforts. Nuclear weapons, as we've been discussing, have been sustained by the theory of deterrence, resulting in one of the greatest arms races the world has ever known. The theory of nuclear deterrence, however, is basically the threat of nuclear retaliation, which compounds the problem by justifying expanding nuclear arsenals. Deterrence is an intellectually and morally bankrupt exercise that has brought humanity to the brink of disaster. The shallow theory of deterrence continues to put us in peril.

Ikeda: Numerous people once in the forefront of nuclear strategy have clearly demonstrated the same flaws in the theory of nuclear deterrence. Likening them to the sword of Damocles, John F. Kennedy said it is dangerous for human beings to live side by side with nuclear weapons. On several occasions, aircraft with hydrogen bombs onboard have crashed. Nuclear missiles have come perilously close to being launched by mistake. The danger that control-systems glitches could trigger atomic attacks unbeknownst to leaders led Mikhail Gorbachev to halt the arms race with the United States. We now know that, in situations like the Cuban missile crisis and the Vietnam War, U.S. presidents and politicians considered using nuclear weapons. Looking back, we see that nothing but luck—not deterrence—has saved us from another Hiroshima or Nagasaki.

No matter what the rhetoric, relying on nuclear weapons for deterrence is entrusting our right to exist to the rulers (sometimes to military leaders or control systems) of a few nuclear "have" nations. The jeopardy that feeble approach places us in is all too apparent.

The times require a spiritual revolution in leaders as well as in the ordinary people—a revolution that evokes the human power for good, the power that can triumph over nuclear might.

Responsibility Lies With Each of Us

Krieger: The way to alter the political system and generate the political will for abolishing nuclear weapons is to arouse the people to demand such change. If leaders are unwilling to attain the goal on their own, then ordinary people must compel them to find the way out of the Nuclear Age. If the people lead, the politicians will follow. I find this a hopeful possibility.

The nuclear threat is global; it affects every human being on the planet. Therefore, its solution cannot be left in the hands of a few political leaders and their military and security advisors. The responsibility for eliminating nuclear weapons lies with each of us.

Ikeda: That is the vital issue. What Toynbee labeled putting faith in scientific progress amounts to belittling human spirituality.

Josei Toda said: "Science begins with observations of the exterior world, on which life depends. It is therefore capable of thoroughly understanding that external world. But the most exhaustive understanding of the external world cannot ensure real human happiness or the peace of human society. This is why what's needed is an exploration of the inner life of human beings.

"This way of thinking can guide scientific technology correctly and contribute to the peace of the world."[3]

Krieger: We need the external and internal worlds to remain connected. Science divorced from morality threatens the human future.

Eliminating nuclear weapons is a critical issue for democratic action. It is incumbent upon people everywhere to understand that they are responsible and that this issue cannot be delegated to political leadership. Leaders have to take responsible action, but political will arises from the people themselves.

Merely agreeing never to use or test nuclear weapons is insufficient. The only way to assure the safety and security of humanity is to eliminate these weapons entirely. Politicians have tried to placate the people by holding out to them agreements to prevent nuclear proliferation, to stop nuclear testing or to dismantle some nuclear weapons. None of these steps is sufficient to end the threat posed by nuclear weapons.

Ikeda: In spite of various pacts, the threat of nuclear arms remains essentially unchanged.

Krieger: Nuclear weapons represent utter destruction, the antithesis of everything decent. Portable incinerators capable of destroying all life, they reflect the darkest side of the human spirit.

Ikeda: Now that we have nuclear arms technology, aside from technical problems, our most difficult task is achieving humanity-wide consensus renouncing its use forever.

Krieger: To fight against the evil of nuclear weapons, as your mentor, Josei Toda, and many others have urged, is to fight for life. The struggle against them is a struggle for decency, dignity and life itself. The effort required in the struggle ennobles the human spirit.

An Absolute Evil

Ikeda: Your assertion that nuclear arms "reflect the darkest side of the human spirit" is the focal point of Toda's declaration against nuclear weapons.

Krieger: The struggle to eliminate nuclear weapons gives precedence to humanity over materialism and to spirituality over intellectual justifications. It recognizes the trap of deterrence theory, of believing that security is attainable at the cost of threatening to incinerate whole nations. The outcome of such belief is not security but the utter corruption of the human spirit. It demonstrates the peril of subordinating the spirit to the intellect.

Ikeda: Nuclear weapons threaten our right to exist and are an absolute evil. Unless we rid the world of them, peace will remain an illusion. Forty-five years ago, in his declaration against them, Toda clearly identified the true nature of nuclear weapons not from the standpoint of ideology but from that of all human life.

"I insist," he said, "that anyone in any nation anywhere, victorious or defeated, who would use nuclear weapons should be condemned to death. We the peoples of the earth have the right to live. Anyone who threatens that right is a demon, a Satan, a monster."[4]

Of course, as a Buddhist, Toda opposed capital punishment. He spoke of condemning to death to emphasize the severity of the consequences of the demonic impulse represented by the wish to possess nuclear weapons. He wished to eradicate the evil that makes people want to use them, using the word *death* to underscore the importance of its antonym, *life*.

Krieger: Toda's statement that "the peoples of the earth have the right to live" is an expression of simple decency, which is reflected in the Universal Declaration of Human Rights. Because of its simplicity, some may fail to grasp its wisdom immediately. But wisdom is generally simple.

Ikeda: Toda was a great leader of the people in part because he always explained the essences of things in simple words readily understood by everyone.

The demon he mentions in his declaration can be explained simply. Buddhism describes anything that deprives people of life or destroys their wisdom as *mara*. The so-called devil king of the sixth heaven is the most formidable personification of *mara* and the inner human lust to enslave others. Toda identified nuclear weapons as a product of this sixth heaven. Though they are, of course, the result of scientific progress, he interpreted such weapons as the progeny of negative aspects of human life. Identifying their true essence, he urged us to fight against them to the end.

The devil king is not a being extrinsic to humanity but one that dwells within the minds of all people. This is why the elimination of nuclear weapons requires a spiritual struggle in each person's mind.

Faith in Youth

Krieger: Since the Cold War ended, we are at a crossroads in the movement to abolish nuclear weapons. No dramatic change has occurred in the basic security policies of nations that continue to rely on nuclear weapons for security even though they can no longer identify whom they are attempting to deter.

Opposition to this status quo is growing worldwide. Thus far, however, governments of the nuclear-weapons states have effectively thwarted it. But indefinite prolongation of the current situation is likely to result in nuclear disaster. For this reason, I think Josei Toda's Declaration for the Abolition of Nuclear Weapons retains its importance today, and I am pleased that you are committed to keeping his thoughts alive among the youth of the SGI. I, too, have great faith in youth.

Ikeda: The Chinese writer Lu Xun said that even knowing that one will fade away in the process, it is a joy to give one's blood, drop by drop, to nurture another person. In my contact with Josei Toda, he personified the meaning of those words. And, as his disciple, I share his devotion to training the young.

Krieger: Young people are the future. It is vital that they have a say in the world they are inheriting and play a major part in resolving the nuclear threat.

PART FOUR

THE CHALLENGE OF THE FUTURE

CHAPTER TWELVE

Human Security and the Future of the United Nations

Ikeda: The theme of the Millennium Summit, held in September 2000 — "The Role of the United Nations in the Twenty-first Century" — reflects the urgent need for organizational reform. As you know, having expanded and subdivided dramatically, the UN structure now includes branches for human rights, the environment, development and the economy. Nonetheless, its most basic role remains international peace and security.

Krieger: The United Nations was founded at the end of World War II with the primary goal of ending "the scourge of war." Its founders had lived through two devastating world wars and recognized the need to create an institutional structure at the international level to maintain peace.

Ikeda: Its goal is clearly set forth in the preamble to the UN Charter: "We the peoples of the United Nations determined to save succeeding generations from the scourge of war which twice in our lifetime has brought untold sorrow to mankind...." Emphasis on the subject "We the peoples" and the warm human touch suggested by "our lifetime" reveal the basic UN spirit to be not that of a federation of nation-states but that of an organization representing the sum of all human beings longing for peace. Whatever reforms the United Nations undergoes, the people's will is required in the decision-making processes.

Krieger: But though the Charter begins with the ringing words "We the peoples of the United Nations," in fact, it is not an organization truly *of the people.* It is one *of nations,* and delegates to it represent nations.

Ikeda: Yes, as its name makes explicit, the United Nations took its origins in and still preserves the European nationalism that dates back to 1648 and the Peace of Westphalia.[1]

Krieger: The power of the United Nations resides primarily in the Security Council, which is dominated by five permanent members, the victors in World War II: the United States, the United Kingdom, Russia (formerly the Soviet Union), France and China. Armed with the power of veto, each permanent member can prevent the Security Council from taking action to maintain peace.

For this reason, the United Nations has been ineffectual in keeping the peace. In the decades since World War II, more than 150 wars have cost the lives of more than twenty-five million people. One or more of the permanent members of the Security Council has either dominated or supported most of these wars. The United Nations is caught in a Catch-22 situation in which the perceived national interests of its most powerful members are at odds with the stated goals of the organization.

Ikeda: This problem has plagued the United Nations since the outset. Its very Charter contains contradictions. For instance,

Article 2, Section 1, says, "The Organization is based on the principle of the sovereign equality of all its Members." This means that a small nation with a population of tens of thousands should have the same rights as huge nations like the United States and Russia. Article 27, Section 3, of the Charter, however, gives Security Council members a special privilege by granting them a veto.

Indeed, the pivotal Security Council has performed ineffectually. The UN security role did not garner much attention until about ten years ago.

Krieger: And yet security is the true heart of the UN promise. I have no doubt that the United Nations is needed, even in its present imperfect form. I also have no doubt that the organization is in need of serious reform.

Ikeda: Significantly, while the League of Nations was very short-lived, the United Nations has lasted for more than half a century. It has had its ups and downs, including U.S.-USSR confrontations, oft-voiced comments about its uselessness and its own failures in places like Bosnia and Somalia. Nonetheless, the strong, prayerful popular desire for a world without war has kept it alive this long.

That is why, as a peace-loving citizen, though fully aware of the way it often concentrates on nation-state interests, in everything I do and say, I remain a thoroughgoing UN supporter.[2]

The Need To Abolish War

Krieger: Nuclear weapons are, in a larger sense, embedded in the war system. And it is the war system itself that must be dismantled. In a brief but moving impromptu speech at the

1998 State of the World Forum, Joseph Rotblat said that nuclear weapons abolition is his short-term goal. His long-term goal is the abolition of war itself. The speech was made just days before his ninetieth birthday.

Ikeda: Rotblat, a man whose whole life has been dedicated to peace and science, was the very first recipient of the Toda Prize for Peace Research, instituted to commemorate Toda's centennial. In his acceptance speech, he said that the power of evil cannot conquer evil and that the threat of war cannot avert war.

Krieger: He is absolutely right in insisting on doing away with war. Abolishing nuclear weaponry is critical but not enough. War, this barbaric way of settling disputes, must be abolished as a human institution.

A Peoples Assembly

Ikeda: But achieving that goal is impossible as long as security is centered on the nation-state. The tragic wars of the twentieth century arose out of excessive confidence in the functioning of the nation. The nation is often the guilty party in problems like poverty and human rights. And these problems, which cause war, have transcended the framework of individual nations to affect all of international society. Consequently, the United Nations must make state sovereignty relative, not absolute, while calling fully on the wisdom of the masses. I have consistently voiced this opinion to UN leaders.

Krieger: Actually, new technologies, particularly in the area of communications, are already making state sovereignty gradually less relevant, but the United Nations has been slow to adapt. Change is essential. A useful UN reform would bring into the organization the "peoples" referred to in the Charter Preamble. This could be achieved by setting up, parallel with the General Assembly, a Peoples Assembly composed of representatives of civil society.

Ikeda: Years ago, I proposed just such a Peoples Assembly. Article 71 of the UN Charter qualifies nongovernmental organizations to engage in deliberation and consultation. A Peoples Assembly would give them a bigger role.

Krieger: It would introduce perspectives different from those of nations. It would bring in human concerns in addition to national interests. Establishing a Peoples Assembly would constitute an important step forward for the United Nations.

Ikeda: Setting it up will be difficult. Still the time definitely has come for a system reflecting popular will. We might create a standing World Peoples Council to make full use of NGO information-gathering capacities and on-site experience and submit proposals to the General Assembly for deliberation and consultation.

Krieger: Even creating a Peoples Assembly, though, would not resolve the great problem of abolishing war. Certainly introducing the perspectives of civil society would provide impetus in the right direction, but it would still be necessary to enforce prohibitions against the use of aggressive force. This would require the cooperation of the permanent members of the Security Council, a UN organ in serious need of reform itself. Instead of representing humanity's greater interests, the permanent members continue to reflect Cold War divisions that no longer exist.

Ikeda: The League of Nations failed because it insisted on una-nimity. Trying to learn from the failure, the Security Council favors large countries. But, as is clear to anyone, this approach is already outmoded.

Krieger: Exactly. Changing the composition of the Security Council is a key item for consideration. A modification or elimination of the permanent members' veto power is needed to enable the Council to uphold international law and main-tain peace. But reforming the Security Council and amending the UN Charter present difficult political problems demand-ing a full hearing and the consideration of alternative possi-bilities.

Ikeda: Clearly, Security Council reform requires more than sim-ply discussing whether to give Japan and Germany permanent membership.

Krieger: Indeed it does. In recent years, the possibilities of UN reform have been widely discussed, and many good reports have been issued. At the outset of a new century, the time has come to take action to strengthen the United Nations so it can fulfill its important mandate. As things stand now, instead of being a place where nations and peoples come together to resolve problems of common interest, the United Nations is too often the scene of jockeying by nations for the sake of their own interests. This must change.

Human Security

Ikeda: Since the end of the Cold War, the United Nations has tried to cope with security in a trial-and-error fashion. In general, it has been split into two camps on this score. The hard-power faction opts for strict crisis control and the unhesitating use of armed force against terrorists and any nations that threaten the current international order and value criteria. The other faction opts for what is called *human security*. First introduced in the 1993 *Human Development Report* of the UN Development Program, the concept arose from the process of dealing with nonmilitary problems like development and the environment that pose potential dangers to human life and dignity.

Krieger: Human security requires strong efforts to end the crush of poverty. We need the United Nations to demand such effort of all its members. This is a responsibility of the world community. Some of the environmental problems implied — polluting the oceans and atmosphere, global warming, destroying the ozone layer and exhausting the earth's resources — are global and work to the detriment of present and future generations. In other words, they relate to human security now and in the years to come. We need a forum to address these concerns. If it is not the United Nations, then a new global organization is necessary. The concept of human security can help organize and motivate the United Nations and guide its reform.

Ikeda: Fulfilling the UN role in ensuring human security demands a radical strengthening of its Economic and Social Council. Immediately after the Cold War, the United Nations challenged the concept of pacification by means of military might. The challenge took the form of the so-called peacekeeping forces.

But this approach came to grief in Somalia and Bosnia. In the hope of learning from its mistake, since that time, the United Nations has gradually shifted its emphasis to human security.

Krieger: Human security looks to the individual instead of the nation-state as the subject of concern. It demands protection of the environment and protection against human rights abuses. It demands an end to poverty as well as to war and genocide. It demands an end to the threat of nuclear holocaust. It demands a judicial system capable of holding states and individuals accountable for violations of international law. It demands a system of nonviolent conflict-resolution.

The power of our technologies makes our problems global. No nation by itself can protect its citizens from them. National security now requires common security, just as human security demands global security. Genocide and crimes against humanity anywhere violate human security everywhere. Violence or starvation anywhere threatens human security everywhere. Since we are all interconnected, we need a global organization capable of responding to the common dangers and threats confronting humanity.

Ikeda: It is up to us to make the United Nations such an organization. In the years to come, the SGI will step up its efforts to effect reform leading to participation by the masses. We are strongly aware that a focus on human security can expose the futility of deterrence, which is based on the notion that nuclear weapons are necessary because they exist.

Krieger: That is an important point. In the light of human security, deterrence is selfish, foolish and dangerous. It jeopardizes the whole to protect a part. But if the whole is destroyed, so is the part. If all humanity is destroyed, so is the nation, which would no longer have significance. For the common good, the theory of deterrence should be laid to rest.

National Security Depends Upon Global Security

Ikeda: The concept of national security was obsolete the moment nuclear weapons came into being.

Krieger: In a sense, we are racing against time. By confronting humanity with the possibility of annihilation, the Nuclear Age has made time more precious and meaningful. Consequently, the United Nations, as a force countervailing this power of destruction, is precious and meaningful. Those who dismiss it as irrelevant dismiss our best chance to face and resolve the threats to human security inherent in the Nuclear Age.

The United Nations must be reformed and made strong enough to face the challenges of our time. National military structures and resorting to arms are likely to exist as long as inequitable distribution of global resources results in poverty, suffering and premature death for large numbers of the world's people. If we make the United Nations democratic and empower it to legislate, adjudicate and enforce international law, we will move toward a more equitable world where human security receives top priority.

Ikeda: Achieving that kind of world, which we all hope for, requires repeated, persevering and honest debate on the best way to strike a balance between national authority and UN authority.

Krieger: Ironically, the nations most insistent on democracy at the national level seem least inclined to democratize the United Nations. The greatest detractors of the United Nations are the strongest supporters of national sovereignty. They look to a past era when national sovereignty may have been sufficient to assure national security. This is no longer the case. As we have noted, powerful technologies have made national security dependent upon global security, and global security demands elements of sovereignty at the global level. The United Nations needs enough authority to meet the challenges of ending war and providing for human security. If individual citizens of the world are to entrust sovereignty to it, even indirectly through their nations, the United Nations has to become a more democratic, global organization.

Education for World Citizenship

Ikeda: To round out our discussion of UN reform, I would like to say: No matter how the organization may be changed, it is always human beings who operate it. Human beings define their identity in various terms, such as their family, their neighborhood, society at large, their nation and the entire world. A loss of identity has accompanied the end of the Cold War as well as economic and informational globalization and has been at the root of recent ethnic conflicts. Though requiring patience, surely the best way to generate deep-rooted support for UN reform is to inspire people to place the highest value on being world citizens.

When I spoke with Boutros Boutros-Ghali in 1997, he expressed concern that people may become isolationist as a backlash against globalization. To counteract this requires cultivating people who, while contributing to the welfare of their local regions, remain constantly aware of their world citizenship.

Krieger: Education for world citizenship is an essential step in building a foundation for human security.

CHAPTER THIRTEEN

Literature
and Life

Ikeda: Good literature has enriched my life. Reading expands our worldview and gives us perspectives on world citizenship. It enables us to engage in dialogue with strangers from all regions and times. It lets us visit unknown lands. A philosopher spoke wisely when he said the people of a bookless house are soulless.

When I was a young man, World War II had just ended. Life was hard for the people of Japan, who had lost their spiritual mainstays. The collapse of old values had plunged us into a spiritual vacuum. In my search for the optimum way to live, I turned to books, both modern and ancient, from all over the world. Books were my best friends. Although times were hard, I haunted secondhand bookstores and read voraciously. I read works by Goethe, Dante, Hugo, Dostoevsky and Tolstoy over and over again. I recall with fondness the neighborhood group we formed to study and discuss what we were reading, and I owe my current ability to lecture, write and engage in dialogues with intellectuals from all parts of the globe to those youthful experiences.

Krieger: Reading is life-expanding. It can put us in touch with people who lived thousands of years ago and enable us to contemplate possible futures for humanity. Through reading we can learn the perspectives of individuals from cultures we have never witnessed. In a sense, reading creates the possibility of carrying on dialogues across time and space.

Merits and Demerits of the Image Culture

Ikeda: Josei Toda always urged us young people to will ourselves to make time for the spiritual richness of contemplation and serious reading. He considered the heart fundamental. He never missed an opportunity to inquire about what I was reading. I, too, now take every chance to urge young people to read good books. Reading in youth deepens the spirit and provides rich nourishment for personality formation.

Krieger: You are fortunate to have had a mentor who took an interest in what you read and helped direct you toward important literature. Such is not the case for many young people now. Electronic entertainment replaces reading for much of today's youth. I find this a serious problem in several ways. First, television overflows with violence. For some reason, violent behavior provides an easy form of television entertainment. I am afraid that, having grown up witnessing so many violent acts on television, children come to take violence for granted, as part of their lives. In the case of video games, children actually participate in simulated violence. I doubt this reflects a healthy society.

Ikeda: Japanese young people today tend to be more familiar with electronic images than with books, and their apparent aversion to reading causes concern. Their reactions to the outside world are entirely passive. It is distressing that they seem to be undergoing a hollowing-out of the spirit, content to live for momentary pleasures. This is unfortunate for both the individual youth and the future of the whole nation. Swept along by material plenty, young people give up their independence. This is why I seek to cultivate in youth the habits of reading and thinking for themselves.

Reading Tempers the Imagination

Krieger: Television leaves little to the imagination. Reading, on the other hand, gives a child word pictures that are converted into images in the mind. Imagination provides us with potential alternatives. It is a primary ingredient in creativity. Inevitably the shift away from reading restricts imagination and lessens creative alternatives. This is unhealthy for both the individual and society.

Ikeda: When I was growing up, there was no television. We were not inundated with information. To obtain knowledge, we had to turn to books. I saved my small allowance to buy books and spent as much time as possible reading. The limited kinds and numbers of books available to us then meant that often I read the same books several times. After I started earning my own money, not a day went by without my picking up a book to read. The dialogues I had with authors on life and philosophy tempered my own powers of contemplation. I memorized outstanding literary or profoundly insightful passages. As time went by, I gradually challenged myself to read increasingly serious works.

Passive acceptance of whatever information television provides robs young people of the desire for intellectual challenge; it deprives them of critical spirit. In your terms, it restricts their creative alternatives.

Krieger: Television is technology for passive learning. Almost by definition, watching it is a form of laziness. TV feeds us information, often of a very superficial sort. It rarely challenges the viewer to think. It has been a means for reducing drama to the mundane. Spiritual decay in modern societies goes deeper than TV and the decline in reading good literature; nonetheless, these factors contribute to our malaise.

Ikeda: If, as you say, television reduces drama to the mundane, it also exalts some people and events above their merits. As is the case with entertainment idols, merely appearing on TV seems to impart something extraordinary.

Krieger: Television can give an appearance of importance to what is actually very shallow. As a medium of communication, television seems to promote celebrity for its own sake.

Ikeda: Television also exerts a great influence on politics and politicians. Some have taken full advantage of this influence, as Kennedy did in his televised debates with Nixon. Politicians concern themselves with being telegenic. Indeed, their looks become an important factor in political strategies. Society needs the ability to discern the ways TV manipulates them and public opinion. Without due vigilance in watching over the media, we can easily find ourselves falling prey to what has been called "Fascism with a smile."

Krieger: Television has also served as a means of electronic colonialism, leading to the Hollywood-ization of values. It has been a vehicle for spreading Western—particularly American —values throughout the world. It has put a strong emphasis on the material as opposed to the spiritual. It has also undermined some very ancient, decent cultural values and instead has stressed violence, alienation and the pursuit of power. On the whole, television helps homogenize the world. And this, too, is dangerous for the future of humanity.

Ikeda: Undeniably, some TV material is worthwhile. In this age of advancing multimedia technology, including the Internet, the idea of doing away with television altogether is impractical. To use television in ways that create value we must be resolutely independent, which, in turn, requires us to cultivate the power to think and temper ourselves spiritually through reading.

Krieger: I think you have gotten to the heart of the problem. If we take human independence seriously, we will educate young people and use our communication media to encourage and develop independent thinking. What specifically do you encourage young people to read?

Studying the Classics

Ikeda: I recommend the famous works and classics of world literature, especially the longer novels, which collectively express much of humanity's intellectual heritage and exhibit a deep insight into human nature. As I have said, I was especially fond of reading Goethe, Dante, Hugo, Dostoevsky and Tolstoy; but there are many other excellent writers as well. Instead of recommending things to read, I prefer to stimulate young people to read widely according to their own tastes and to discover books and writers that appeal strongest to them. Vague recommendations of authors and books have little effect on the many young people averse to the act of reading. This is why, at every opportunity, I try to stimulate interest by giving actual examples of the contents and language of good books.

Who are your favorite writers? What authors made the
deepest impression on you in your youth?

Krieger: Among the many writers I enjoy are Albert Camus,
Erich Maria Remarque, Mark Twain and Kurt Vonnegut. I like
powerful drama, but I also like humor and irreverence, which
are excellent at puncturing hypocrisy and arrogance. Twain,
Vonnegut and Joseph Heller all have this kind of irreverence.
My favorite poet is Pablo Neruda. He had a poetic gift for
expressing great passion in a very few words. This is the gift
of a great poet.

Hemingway, Fitzgerald and Steinbeck all made strong im-
pressions on me in my late teens and early twenties. I enjoyed
Tolstoy and Dostoevsky, too. I have read several Japanese
authors—including Akutagawa, Kawabata, Mishima and Oe
—and found them very powerful.

Much of my reading today concerns my work and is related
to international law and nuclear disarmament. In these areas,
Richard Falk and Jonathan Schell have written very well
indeed. Still, I try to read novels when I have a chance. I
recently read Vonnegut's newest novel and reread several of his
earlier works.

Ikeda: The act of reading outstanding literature is essential to
human development—it moves, purifies and elevates the soul.
General Douglas MacArthur once asked Prime Minister Shigeru Yoshida why Japanese generals of their own day were
inferior to generals of the late nineteenth and early twentieth
centuries (the Meiji period, 1867–1912). Yoshida asked Tetsu-
ro Watsuji, a professor at Tokyo University, for his opinion
on the matter. Watsuji said it was because Japanese generals
used to study the classics, whereas modern generals were

educated only in their fields of specialty. Because they made no effort to study the classics, they lacked resolve.[1] The same can be said about many people in positions of leadership today.

Josei Toda used Thomas Henry Hall Caine's *The Eternal City* and the famous Chinese novel *The Water Margin* in teaching youth the whole scope of life, including the nature of friendship, how to interpret humanity and theories of organization and revolution.

It seems to me that readers today are often solely seeking information. They even read masterpieces merely to know the stories and claim familiarity with celebrated literary works. Few aim to engage in dialogue with authors or to cultivate their own minds.

Krieger: That is a great shame. Reading, as you say, offers the possibility of engaging with great and noble minds. It has helped me to understand the power of the written word and to learn from those who have gone before, as well as from my contemporaries.

The Blessing of Life-Changing Books

Ikeda: I advise young people to read the great works that permit them to become part of a shared humanity-wide culture. By reading great Japanese literature you have learned something about the culture and attitudes of the people of Japan.

Though it is said to be especially difficult to translate, Japanese literature is nonetheless becoming familiar worldwide thanks to outstanding translators and literary scholars. I hope the number of translations will grow so that people everywhere can learn more about Japan and the Japanese.

Krieger: Japan has many great writers and a rich culture. The Japanese concepts of beauty are particularly subtle and important.

I have always considered good writing a gift from the author to the world, a gift from one soul to another. I have found that reading a good book nourishes my soul and gives me joy and hope.

Ikeda: In his fourteenth-century work *Tsurezuregusa* (Essays in idleness), Yoshida Kenko said reading is "making friends with people from an invisible world." His sentiment resembles your idea of learning from people who have gone before.

In addition, reading is dialogue with oneself; it is self-reflection, which cultivates profound humanity. Reading is therefore essential to our development. It expands and enriches the personality like a seed that germinates after a long time and sends forth many blossom-laden branches.

People who can say of a book "this changed my life" truly understand the meaning of happiness. Reading that sparks inner revolution is desperately needed to escape drowning in the rapidly advancing information society. Reading is more than intellectual ornamentation; it is a battle for the establishment of the self, a ceaseless challenge that keeps us young and vigorous.

Krieger: It saddens me that more young people have not discovered the pleasure of reading and the expanded horizons reading can offer. I love your concept of "a dialogue with oneself." Reading can spark this dialogue by stimulating us with new ideas and challenging our old patterns of thinking. Reading can take us across and even erase borders. It should be a treasured path to world citizenship.

Poetry: An Expression of the Soul

Ikeda: Poetry manifests the human spirit; it is an artistic expression of faith, an irrepressible outflowing of the human soul with energy to move the minds of others. Superior poetic works lift the reader's spirit, inspiring reverence for cosmic rhythms and ingenuous nature. Poetry can also be a call to resist oppression. The hearts of poets, embodied in their words, arouse sympathetic vibrations in readers' minds.

In *Leaves of Grass*, Walt Whitman — one of my personal favorites — transcended the conventional poetic diction of the past to give voice to a naked human cry. The book, which I read many times in my youth, always impressed me as a hymn to the New World, an expression of devout faith, an indictment of hypocrisy and declaration of sympathy for the ordinary working people.

Krieger: Good poetry touches the human spirit. It reminds us of who we are and reawakens us to the mystery of our lives. So much of day-to-day life concerns what we possess or want to possess. It is all very material. But what we have is not who we are. The American political scientist Harold Laswell defined his field as the study of who gets what, when and how. None of the sciences, social or physical, can really tell us much about who we are or why we exist. Nor can they tell us much about being courageous, decent and loving. These issues pertain to the human spirit and are at the heart of good poetry.

Reviving the Spirit of Poetry

Ikeda: More than anything else, world leaders today need to rehabilitate the poetic spirit in order to halt the hollowing-out of the spirit and the devastation caused by ever-expanding ego and greed.

The poetic spirit can take many forms. I'm sure you remember this incident that occurred in America during the Vietnam War. Armed soldiers were called out to halt an antiwar demonstration. A young woman demonstrator stepped up to a bayonet-wielding soldier and presented him with a single flower. Her gift symbolized her faith in the soldier's goodness of heart. Surely this was an expression of the poetic spirit.

Krieger: That is a wonderful example. I remember a photo of a courageous young woman placing a flower in the barrel of a soldier's rifle. Her gesture was a simple, symbolic act. But it was also poetic and raised profound questions: Which was more powerful, the flower or the rifle? Who was more courageous, the young woman or the armed soldier? What united and what divided these two young people, soldier and protester, the servant of the state and the citizen? These questions reflect on who we are and why we live.

The Poetry of Peace

Ikeda: The poetic spirit encourages people in all ranks and places to return to their naked humanity. Neither sentimental nor fantastic, it embraces and affirms the whole world and all its inhabitants; it imparts the will to remain optimistic and unbending in the face of all hardships.

As a believer in innate human goodness, I am certain that the concentrated power of good can overcome the greatest forces of evil. The poetic spirit helps us control the greed-dominated self. It helps us handle the actual while keeping our eyes turned toward the ideal.

Without the poetic spirit, we cannot counter the mechanizing effects of the nation-state system and its authoritarian theories; we cannot achieve lasting peace. Peace movements lacking in poetic spirit become mechanized and susceptible to authoritarianism.

Mahatma Gandhi understood this well. He advocated nonviolence because he saw the futility of trying to fight violence with violence. His nonviolent movement embodies a great poetic spirit.

Krieger: Human beings are not just numbers. We are not just statistics to be studied in the aggregate and manipulated. Nevertheless, the political process often seems to treat us as if we were. Polls are conducted on every imaginable issue, and so-called leaders moderate their public statements to match polling results. True leadership, however, demands vision and connections with the human spirit. Gandhi and King had these, so do Havel and Mandela. Standing far above their contemporaries, these men have been poets of politics.

For a long time I have believed the world needs poets who are political leaders and political leaders who are poets. Particularly in Latin America, this has been a tradition. Neruda, for example, was Chilean ambassador to France. Many individuals who hold no political office have entered on the world stage performing profoundly poetic acts that are political, too.

Ikeda: Unfortunately, not many Japanese politicians or high-ranking officials have been poets. For that matter, ordinary citizens are often too obsessed with mundane business to perform poetic actions.

The Japanese poet Kotaro Takamura said that, instead of picking up gold from among roadside rubbish, the poet understands that the rubbish itself is gold in disguise.

Krieger: Rosa Parks' act of defiance in refusing to give up her seat to a white man on a bus in Montgomery, Alabama, in 1955 touched the poetic spirit. By her determination to hold her ground, she said, wordlessly, "I too am a human being entitled to equal dignity with all other human beings." When King said, "I have a dream," he was speaking to the human spirit in the language of poetry.

I believe a poem is far less important than is the poet. We all seek a voice. Sometimes that voice speaks in words, sometimes in acts. The poetic voice always explores the mystery of who we are and takes a firm stand for human dignity. Such a voice — such poetry — always carries hope.

Ikeda: Rosa Parks is an example of a courageous woman of action. True poetry is not confined to the ivory tower of calm meditation. Only the spirit made profound by action and self-struggle can spin poetry that touches the heart.

More than mere assemblages of words, as I have said, poetry is the expression of the spirit. This is why it touches a sympathetic chord with humanity, with all life and with the whole universe. Even the actions of people who leave no written record can be great poetry.

I started writing poetry when I was young and from time to time still compose and dedicate to others both long and short verses. The Japanese poet Bin Ueda once said that poetry is motivated by what he called the three Ws: War, Women and Wine. People have said that my poetry is devoted to the three Ps: Peace, People and Philosophy.

I agree with you that the poet is more important than the poem. What poets do you like best and why?

Poetry That Is Alive

Krieger: I love poetry that is alive, that teaches me something about who I am as a human being. I am strongly drawn to Spanish-language poets. Their imagery is very vivid, and their associations are often surprising and fresh. Neruda is my favorite. I also like Jorge Luis Borges and Federico Garcia Lorca. They exhibit a spirit of protest and, to the core of their beings, are committed to human dignity. I find them to be brave and honorable, with great gifts of expression.

I am also drawn to poets in other languages who exhibit the same characteristics. Among Americans, I enjoy the poetry of Robert Bly, Denise Levertov and Philip Levine, all of whom challenge war. During the Vietnam War each of them, through their poems, placed flowers in soldiers' rifles.

Ikeda: All three seem to embody the three Ps and to devote their lives to their convictions. Reducing life to a mere means, war denies its supreme value. No poet worthy of the name should affirm war. You, however, are a peace warrior richly endowed with the spirit of poetry. I have been deeply moved by the several wonderful poems you have given me. Surely your love of poetry is connected with your pacifist work.

Krieger: I believe both peace and poetry arise from the same core of yearning and profound respect for human dignity.

For reasons different from the ones I mentioned earlier, I also enjoy good haiku, which provide flash insights into the human spirit.

Ikeda: I, too, am fond of haiku and the conciseness with which they express the season and symbolize the world of the heart.

Krieger: I especially like the poems of Matsuo Basho, Yosa Buson and Kobayashi Issa. Each was connected not only with the earth and its various life forms but also with the entire universe. For me, haiku reinforces the aesthetic of simplicity. I find it much more satisfying than dense, flowery verse. I especially like this one by Issa:

> *The world of dew is only a world of dew*
> *And yet —*
> *And yet —*

Although said to reflect Issa's personal grief and misery, this haiku conveys the possibility of something more, of hopefulness. The repeated "and yet" suggests the ever-present possibility of a better tomorrow. How we take advantage of the possibility is up to us.

The Social Role of Literature

Ikeda: Now I should like to turn our attention to the social role of literature in general. Jean-Paul Sartre once asked what literature can do for starving children.[2] Of course, literature cannot appease hunger. But I think Sartre was less interested in pointing up literature's impotence in dealing with poverty than in arousing the literati to an awareness of their social mission.

In addition to its social mission, literature plays an important part in the individual search for understanding and fulfillment. During World War II in Japan, college graduation dates were rushed so that graduates could be mobilized as fast as possible. Many young soldiers kept books by their sides to the very end, pouring over them to discover meaning in their circumstances. Realizing that people cannot live by bread alone, they were urgently concerned with spiritual hunger.

Would you agree that literature is an indispensable source of spiritual nourishment?

Krieger: I value it very highly. Literature is really only a fancy word for storytelling with pen and paper (nowadays, with word processors). Authors of fiction create characters that interact and resolve conflicts both within themselves and among others. Great literature teaches us what being human means and allows us to explore the dimensions of the human spirit through the thoughts and acts of others.

Literature can provide a laboratory for studying human behavior and the human spirit. It allows us to climb inside another person's skin and understand what being that person is like. It allows us to see the world and wrestle with problems in the way another person—a fictional character—does. We can learn from the struggles of others. We can also identify with literary characters in ways that help shape our own actions.

Ikeda: From Homer to modern times, literature has helped the human spirit grow. Great literature profoundly explores such themes as wisdom, the nature of ideal society, greatness and folly, and the human condition in general. This is why people still read the classics.

Krieger: If young people read more great literature and reflected on it as part of their education, wars would be less likely. They would better understand the essential commonality of humans across all cultures. Reading can teach them the truth about and brutality of warfare and the totally unheroic action of killing other human beings. Young men particularly would be less inclined to allow themselves to be used as soldiers.

Ikeda: Literature that works to refine, deepen and save the human soul is akin to a religion that elevates and binds people together. And the texts of great religions, such as the Bible and the Buddhist scriptures, make great literature. Literature and religion are parts of the human heritage, and determining how to use that heritage is essential to our further growth as human beings.

Krieger: This is another rich area for discussion. The great heritage of the world's religions has too often been used in narrow and cynical ways to undermine rather than foster human dignity and to foment wars. Institutionalization has often twisted the core messages of religions and at times robbed them of their very heart and soul. Great literature and poetry, both within and outside a religious context, explore and illuminate our human struggle and provide models of the triumph of the human spirit.

CHAPTER FOURTEEN

The Importance of Nongovernmental Organizations

Ikeda: As indicated by the UN Millennium Forum, held May 2000 in New York, the role of NGOs in international society has been elevated. Indeed this role has expanded dramatically as the United Nations developed. Organizations for independent civic action emerged in almost every field as early as the 1970s. According to some data, in 1909,[1] NGOs numbered a mere 176. By 1998, that number had grown to more than twenty-three thousand. Expanding their grass-roots networks, these organizations contribute greatly to peace and arms reduction and to solving an array of global problems including the environment, development, human rights and other humanitarian issues. Their efforts have grown especially conspicuous since the end of the Cold War.

Krieger: NGOs are civil society in action. Unrestrained by the often narrow self-interests of governments, NGOs can bring the conscience of the global community to bear on serious problems that transcend territorial boundaries. The so-called Earth Summit on environmental issues held in Rio de Janeiro in 1992 was an important turning point in their efforts.

Ikeda: Unlike earlier similar conferences, the Earth Summit opened its doors wide to NGOs. Their participation was recognized from the preparatory stage, and they conducted a Global Forum parallel with the main conference of governmental representatives. The revolutionary management system making this possible was called the UNCED Process after the UN Conference on the Environment and Development, the official conference designation. The same management system was used in a series of UN conferences held during the 1990s on such topics as human rights, population, women and housing.

Krieger: The Earth Summit did a great deal to awaken international society to the power of NGOs. Many of these organizations had already made important contributions on their own. But both on the domestic and international fronts, governments had largely ignored them. The Earth Summit changed that.

Ikeda: Before the conference opened, Maurice Strong, Earth Summit secretary-general, commented on the importance of NGOs in educating and informing the public. He added that governments move into action when the public applies pressure — in the good sense — on them. You have acutely observed the futility of relying on governments and have said that we can achieve peace and respect for human rights only through popular solidarity that compels governments to act.

Krieger: I believe this strongly. NGOs have a different orientation toward the world than governments. They are not bound by the same restrictions as governments, which tend to view the world through lenses of national interests. And national interests often do not coincide with human security. NGOs, on the other hand, generally take a broader and more humane perspective. Their concerns are not limited by national boundaries and interests. This gives them greater freedom to take moral, and global, stands. NGOs can represent the poor, the dispossessed and even future generations. This gives them tremendous moral power.

Ikeda: An important point. As you say, concentrating on national interests relegates the poor to a position of secondary or even tertiary significance and can overlook future generations entirely. NGOs at the grass-roots level are essential if we are to hear ordinary people's voices.

You are an advisor to the highly unusual group called Kids Can Free the Children, a global NGO run by young people to save underprivileged children from forced labor and exploitation. The idea of children getting the help they need from those near them in age has resonated with people around the world. We need more such movements that heed the voices of people in every walk of life and that act and speak for those people.

Moreover, it is crucial that governments listen humbly to NGOs. This is really the way to bring democracy to full maturity within each nation.

NGOs Represent the Interests of Ordinary People

Krieger: I am very proud of my association with Kids Can Free the Children. It was founded and is led by two remarkable young brothers, Craig and Marc Kielburger. Through their humanity, which transcends borders, they have created a great organization of children responding to the needs of other children.

NGOs provide a counterforce to the power of national governments, most of which have usurped greater powers than the people have given them. In a sense, governments misappropriate sovereignty from the people and then use it in ways that may be detrimental to the people's welfare. National governments are influenced by powerful economic forces, corporate and individual, that do not coincide with the people's interests. So long as financial contributions remain at the heart of democratic politics, politicians will feel obliged to give their benefactors more support than they give to the interests of the people.

NGOs are an alternative to governments for specific issues. They provide a place for individuals to transfer allegiance and sovereignty to humanity. More and more individuals are choosing this alternative in relation to human rights, disarmament, development, peace, environment, population and other critical issues.

Ikeda: We can no longer ignore the existence of NGOs in important international decision-making processes. In the areas you cite, NGOs can contribute in more flexible and appropriate ways than national governments can. In addition, they are likely to obey the absolute imperative of respecting human dignity.

Only when ordinary people manifest their independent powers can there be a society in which we all live truly humane lives. Genuine security depends on our determination never to overlook the need for respecting the dignity of each person.

Krieger: NGOs have often come into being because an individual or a few committed people have recognized problems inadequately addressed by governments. In some cases, governments themselves are the problem because they permit human rights abuses or environmental damage or pursue national security policies that jeopardize human security.

NGOs frequently begin with a few dedicated people

organizing themselves to address a specific problem. When they speak out and act, others hear about the problem. Most of these organizations grow in this way; that is, by word of mouth.

Ikeda: The courageous action of one person can be the driving force. Like a stone thrown in the water, it generates ripples of sympathetic reaction.

The Power of Commitment and Compassion

Krieger: That is how NGOs grow and gain support from more and more people. They are rarely well-funded—certainly not in comparison with governments—but they are driven by the power of commitment and compassion. In terms of resources, NGOs are as different from governments as David was from Goliath. Often against tremendous odds, they battle for a better world. They have achieved some impressive results, but most impressive to me is their willingness to struggle against powerful forces for what they believe is right. Their growing power gives hope that important changes can be made on behalf of humanity.

Ikeda: The International Campaign to Ban Landmines is a good case in point. Jody Williams, the founding coordinator, who won the 1997 Nobel Peace Prize, said this about the power of NGOs: "Together we are a superpower. It's a new definition of superpower. It's not one of us; it's all of us."[2]

In my view, her definition of a superpower signifies qualitative excellence instead of quantitative might. Its most salient characteristic is not imposed hegemony but a powerful solidarity.

Krieger: Her words impressed me, too. If people join together, they can generate the power to effectively confront even superpower states. By combining forces with others of like mind, global grass-roots movements of unprecedented strength can arise.

Ikeda: In December 1995, Jan Øberg of Sweden, director of the Transnational Foundation for Peace and Future Research, spoke to me of the need to abandon the thinking that governments are sovereign while the people are subordinate. He also said that, instead of the term *nongovernmental organizations,* which carries the negative prefix *non,* we should adopt the more straightforward designation *people's organizations.* In fact, this would be more suitable to the current times.

The Sovereignty of Conscience

Krieger: I agree that the people must be sovereign. And sovereignty begins with each individual. Every person on earth has the sovereignty of conscience. It is our uniquely human quality. We can each stand up for what we believe is right and refuse to submit to what we know is wrong. Although we can give over part of our sovereignty to a community or nation, we cannot remain fully human and give away to any group — even to a nation — our sovereignty of conscience.

Ikeda: Milton wrote:

> *Merciful over all his works, with good*
> *Still overcoming evil, and by small*
> *Accomplishing great things — by things deemed weak*
> *Subverting worldly strong and worldly wise* [3]

By "worldly strong," I believe he means the power of authority that causes war and tragedy. Human spiritual strength can defeat that authority. Inherent in human life is the strength of hope that can pioneer an epoch of peace.

Buddhism teaches that at every moment life embodies the fundamental power to reform the self, human society and the world. The SGI's concept of human revolution can become the source of the new superpower our age requires, the basis for a broad solidarity based on evoking and pooling each individual's power.

The Power of an Individual

Krieger: The possibilities inherent in people power are limitless, but education is needed for us to recognize them. Most people are caught up in the struggle to survive or to improve their lot. Not many really understand the tremendous power inherent in their lives, and even fewer actually tap into that power.

Gandhi exemplified the power inherent in each of us. He tapped into it and lived with great courage. He was willing to die for what he believed in and often engaged in life-threatening long fasts, which emphasized his commitment to achieve his goals. In the end, the British Empire could not withstand the power of this one man of conscience. Of course, Gandhi's power grew as people throughout India and the world realized the justness of his vision and joined him in seeking to end colonial rule in India.

The power of one strong-willed, courageous, committed individual to prevail over the British Empire suggests what the power of people mobilized in a just cause can accomplish. I gather this is what you mean by each moment of life embodying the power to reform the world.

Ikeda: Correct. As Gandhi's actions demonstrated, what one person can do, everyone can do. During the nonviolent 1930 campaign against the British salt tax, Gandhi said that someone with resolute faith had to get things started. His bravery transmitted itself to the people and brought results. Those who saw him were inspired to follow him and to move forward. Each step he took engendered popular anger against colonialism and strengthened popular resolve to attain independence.

Convinced as he was that true independence is impossible unless the people are spiritually independent, Gandhi put steel in the popular backbone.

Krieger: The possibility of each moment transforming the world suggests that we are far more powerful than we think. Undoubtedly releasing our power requires courage—the courage to be different, to stand apart, to stand up for what we believe is right.

Commitment and compassion, when combined with courage, can change the world. These are the characteristics of the leaders whom I respect most—leaders like Gandhi, King and Mother Teresa.

The Work of Education

Ikeda: This discussion reminds me of French philosopher Blaise Pascal's comment: "Justice without might is helpless; might without justice is tyrannical. Justice without might is gainsaid.... We must then combine justice and might and, for this end, make what is just strong, or what is strong just."[4]

Pascal's topic represents a dilemma with which humanity has always struggled. Learning from history, in the face of the World War II militarism that plagued Japan, Tsunesaburo Makiguchi kept the banner of justice and humaneness aloft. He said: "The instinct of self-preservation makes the evil person cooperate with others immediately. The good person is always alone and weak in the face of evil people who oppress goodness the more powerful they grow.... That is why good people have no recourse but to unite."[5] Once he had arrived at this conclusion, Makiguchi dedicated himself entirely to education. His determination to see the battle for peace, and the people, through to victory inspired the establishment of Soka University as a training ground for truly courageous people —what we Japanese call "true lions."

Krieger: Undeniably education plays a critical role in instilling compassion and commitment in people. When compassion and commitment are linked with courage, the three together constitute a foundation for nonviolence. Some political and military leaders are courageous and committed. But, as long as they fail to link these admirable traits to compassion—as few do—they remain trapped in the cycle of violence.

To break from this cycle and build a better society, requires that we, as you say, reinforce the solidarity of good people. A necessary step to this end is finding ways for NGOs working in different areas to join their efforts. For example, nuclear weapons abolition is not just a disarmament or peace issue. It is also an environmental issue, a human rights issue, an economic issue and a justice issue.

Ikeda: Of course. By their nature, nuclear arms threaten human dignity. At the same time they are a grave threat to the global environment. No one on the planet is unaffected by this threat.

We Must Unite

Krieger: And that is why it is necessary for us to unite. By coming together we can convince ever-widening circles of people that nuclear arms abolition is an issue that affects their futures.

As the numbers grow, the strength actually needed to achieve abolition will also grow.

In my experience, awakening people to the need for nuclear weapons abolition has not been easy. Most people prefer not to think about it. And it is hard to blame them. Confronted with many other pressing problems, they have trouble focusing on whether deterrence really makes sense. People tend to acquiesce until government leaders prove themselves unreliable or untrustworthy. Given this tendency to compliance, changing the status quo is difficult. To achieve it requires imagination and appropriate actions, helping people imagine the utter destructiveness of nuclear weapons use and then taking actions to assure that such destruction never occurs.

Ikeda: The more reluctant people are to think about these vital issues, the more urgent the need to awaken them to things they would prefer to ignore. Lagging in this task could spell the extinction of the human race.

Krieger: The abolition movement is growing because an increasing number of people can now imagine the consequences of nuclear weapons being used again. Still, we have not yet reached the critical mass of people needed to pressure governments to change their policies.

But I believe in the power of the individual and of the human conscience. The world will change when the number of those united to seek a better world by nonviolent means—with liberty, justice and dignity for all—reaches critical mass. This is certainly related to your concept of the human revolution.

Ikeda: Yes. As history shows, good people have always been isolated from each other. Without a sound power base, just actions in the name of social reform have often been frustrated. I am eager to stem this unfortunate tide in human history. If things remain unaltered, our sense of impotence and resignation will increase to where we lose forever all opportunity to rally the courage and wisdom to confront crises boldly.

SGI promotes peace, culture and education based on Buddhist principles. I have long defined its social mission in the following way: To use the spirit arising from the depths of life to struggle against all external restricting forces—violence, authority, financial power and so on—that violate human dignity.

Our situation may be difficult, but standing idly by is unacceptable. The challenge of twenty-first century humanity is to show how mighty people power can be. It is our task to make recognition of that power the hallmark of the age.

CHAPTER FIFTEEN

The Role
of Education

Ikeda: We now face a period of great transition. Whether we can make the twenty-first century a century of peace depends entirely on human will. Humanity has already paid too high a price in repeated tragedies. Let us heed the lesson of the twentieth century—dubbed the century of war and violence—and resolutely put a stop to this tragic course.

Krieger: To achieve this, humanity must change. More compassion and courage are required of us, the courage to live peacefully. The creation of nuclear weapons changed history. If we perpetuate historical trends and continue settling our differences with wars that call on all available technological means, humanity faces a bleak future and possibly no future. It is sobering to realize that humanity has reached the point at which it can destroy itself as a biological species.

There is much good in human beings. We are capable of love, kindness, compassion, sharing, joy, creation and appreciation. All these are worth preserving as is humanity itself.

If we are capable of imagining it, we have the capacity to create a future of human decency. To do so will require us initially to control our most dangerous technologies and then to agree upon new ways to resolve our conflicts without resorting to violence. In other words, we must first abolish nuclear weapons and then abolish war. Abolishing nuclear weapons is a step into the unknown but also a step back from the brink of disaster. Abolishing war requires finding solutions to the causes of war.

These new steps for humankind will be far more important than the first steps on the moon. Stepping on the moon was a technological feat. Stepping back from the brink of disaster and abolishing nuclear weapons and war will require courage and global cooperation beyond anything ever demonstrated in the past.

Ikeda: The greatest gift we can bequeath to future generations is our determination to maintain such courage and cooperation as well as the wisdom to act upon it.

Krieger: As you imply, we need unified human will to move beyond our present historical impasse. This will require leadership and perseverance. The way to create the political will for change is first to create the public support for change. Education of the public is necessary both as to the seriousness of our problems and to foster the belief that solutions are possible. Moreover, an educated public can see through political deceptions and realize that the future is in their hands, that they have the power to generate the political will for change. It will not happen magically. But if those who realize the magnitude of the crisis do everything in their power, they can stimulate the public to act.

The SGI Peace Movement

Ikeda: Precisely. Josei Toda's appeal to rid the world of misery symbolizes the whole Soka Gakkai International peace movement. Our goal is to create a society in which all the evils threatening human dignity have been destroyed and everyone enjoys peace and happiness. It is rooted in the firm conviction that the people themselves are the driving power behind all historical creativity.

One of the many projects SGI has undertaken toward this goal is a series of exhibitions designed to elevate public awareness. In addition to the exhibitions on nuclear arms elimination, we have sponsored exhibitions on such other global issues as human rights and the environment.

Encouraging the Will To Act

Krieger: Such exhibitions play an important role in informing as many people as possible about critical issues, such as the continuing threat of nuclear weapons. When the issues dealt with are crucial, as with the threats to the future of life, courageous recommendations are demanded, which rouse people to act, even in opposition to official positions. Global problems demand global solutions, which require us to help educate the public about the need for global action. Exhibitions can be very valuable because they address particular issues at particular points in time.

Ultimately, people need the capacity to think for themselves and to exercise that capacity to reach intelligent conclusions. For many people, heavy doses of nationalism ("my country, right or wrong") in early education hamper this capacity.

Ikeda: As we discussed earlier, education can plant the seeds of fidelity to national interests. It can also cultivate fidelity to the interests of humanity. You also said that education is the only thing that can empower the people.

Krieger: Yes, and this is why we need peace education to permeate our cultures. We need to reconceptualize history and understand it as more than a series of battles resulting in victories and defeats. And we need more movies, books, dances and plays that explore and promote themes of peace.

Ikeda: Such cultural expressions of peace are the aim of the festivals SGI sponsors all around the world. These events feature singing and other performing arts expressing the importance and wonderful nature of peace. While working on this large scale, we continue more modest dialogue to help the culture of peace take root in communities. Though inconspicuous, this work is also significant. Through undertakings like these, the SGI is accepting the challenge of internalizing peace and building fortresses of peace—as per the UNESCO charter—in the minds of all individuals, who can then spread widely the message of respect for the dignity of all human life.

Krieger: We need to realize and teach that peace is far more than just the absence of war. It is a process of cooperation expressed in every facet of our lives.

Instead of sinking more and more tax money into military establishments, governments should support peace education and devise policies for its promotion. Every high school and college student should be required to take a course in global survival, covering the dangers confronting humanity and creative ways of reducing or ending these dangers. Young people need to learn that they have responsibilities to the community in which they live. Today that community is the global community.

Ikeda: You are describing world-citizen education, which I have long advocated. In fact, I suggested the establishment of a UN

World-Citizen Education Decade. The name is different, but the United Nations did designate the years 2001 to 2010 as the International Decade for a Culture of Peace and Non-Violence for the Children of the World. This is a very significant step. SGI eagerly cooperates with and supports a peace-education–promotion campaign being conducted mainly by UNESCO.

Krieger: Humanity can solve its problems nonviolently. Peace education, inside and outside the classroom, is a source of hope and new possibilities. It is an area where creative, committed and energetic people can truly make a difference in the world. Peace education generates human creativity. Civil society organizations that pool their intelligence and efforts can discover the best ways to enable their education to reach the human heart.

One of the best ways to educate for peace is through student exchanges. When young people travel to and live in other cultures, they learn firsthand about various cultural perspectives. They also learn that people are people everywhere. Both are important lessons. Familiarity with another culture makes it hard to view representatives of that culture abstractly as enemies. Intercultural dialogue is a way to peace.

Hope for Today's Youth

Ikeda: Buddhism teaches equality and absolute respect for the dignity of life. Educating people to be citizens of the world begins with cultivating respect, compassion and empathy for others. I am certain that friendship and limitless trust in people can empower us to overcome socially disruptive discrimination and hatred. As you have implied, open-minded exchanges on the popular level will be increasingly important in the years to come. When people engage in mind-to-mind dialogue, they are grateful to see ethnic and cultural differences not as obstacles but as expressions of society—enriching diversity that engenders respect and a desire for further exploration.

SGI emphasizes the importance of cultural exchanges, especially among young people. Soka University enthusiastically engages in exchange programs with numerous universities throughout the world.

Josei Toda insisted that the passion and power of youth will build a new world. Always with this bold statement in mind, I have exerted my utmost to make the twenty-first century a century of peace. And I strive to be in frequent contact with young people, to observe their growth, and to express my expectations regarding their responsibilities to future generations.

Krieger: Young people have to accept leading roles in the peace movement. Realizing this, we at the Nuclear Age Peace Foundation have instituted a Youth Advisory Council, and we have created a Youth Outreach Coordinator position. I am very hopeful. If people power is the key to changing the status quo, then enlightening young people is the key to strengthening people power for the future.

I would like young people to realize the insanity of living with nuclear weapons, of destroying the environment, of hoarding money while others starve, of settling our differences by killing each other, of dividing ourselves by artificial borders around parcels of earth we call nations. I would like young people to join hands across borders and to insist that their elders do so, too, in order to end our present insanity. In short, I would like young people to choose hope.

Ikeda: The hallmark of youth is optimism and high idealism. The young are constantly challenged to open the door to new eras. Hope is another name for youth, and since this dialogue is called *Choose Hope*, as we near its end, I should like to dedicate to young people this poem by Pablo Neruda, a favorite of both of ours.

What's to be accomplished unless
I bear a part of hope on
My shoulders?
What's to be accomplished unless
I march on, bearing the banner that,
From hand to hand
In the long file of our
Great struggle, has passed
Into my hands? [1]

Krieger: Neruda's poem expresses the responsibility, continuity and the idealism of youth.

Young people have played an active part in all historical transitions. Never before has the challenge confronting the young been greater than today. Never has the need for courageous action been more compelling. My hope is that the youth of the world will see the dangerous chasms dividing us and build bridges across them, bridges that link them to each other and to a better future for all humanity.

In conclusion, I should also like to offer young people some encouragement with this passage from one of my poems:

You are a miracle.
You are a gift of creation to itself.
You are here for a purpose
Which you must find.
Your presence here is sacred and you will
Change the world!

Ikeda: Whether we can make the new century one of symbiosis and hope depends on the extent to which citizens awaken to the needs of the whole human race, expand the circle of global solidarity and work actively within that circle.

What's important is the wisdom of each individual living by a firm philosophy rooted in respect for life. Such wise, ordinary people have the power to halt war and the abuse of authority. Instead of continuing a society dominated by war and violence, our struggle is to build a human republic in which everyone is happy and all are victors. Rather than giving in to fate or circumstances, let us prove our humanity and show its true power as we write a new history of peace. Resolutely and courageously striving to that end indicates that we have chosen hope.

 Notes

Prefaces to the English Edition

1. http://www.walden.org//contemporaries/P/Peabody_Elizabeth
   P/04_War.htm.

2. Arnold Toynbee, *Civilization on Trial*, Oxford University Press, New
   York, 1948, 213.

Chapter One: Peace, Imagination and Action

1. Jonathan Schell, *The Fate of the Earth* (New York: Alfred A. Knopf,
   1982), 119.

2. In 1997, responding to a talk by David Krieger in Tokyo about the
   need to abolish nuclear weapons, the Soka Gakkai youth gathered
   thirteen million signatures in support of abolishing nuclear weapons.
   The petition was presented to the United Nations in October 1998.
   In a second project, the Soka Gakkai youth of Hiroshima and the
   Chugoku region distributed sunflower seeds, symbols of peace.

3. Sheridan Johns, ed. "Speech on Release from Prison," *Mandela, Tambo,
   and the African National Congress: The Struggle Against Apartheid, 1948–1990:
   A Documentary Survey* (New York: Oxford University Press, 1991), 228.
   (Cape Town, February 11, 1990: Upon his release from prison, Mandela quoted from his own 1964 speech following his trial.)

4. Quoted in Charles Birch, *Regaining Compassion for Humanity and Nature*
   (Sydney: New South Wales University Press, 1993), 192. (From a
   May 23, 1946, telegram sent by Albert Einstein to President Roo-
   sevelt on behalf of the Emergency Committee of Atomic Scientists,
   saying in effect that humanity was unprepared to cope with this new
   power.)

5. Nichiren, "Conversation between a Sage and an Unenlightened Man,"
   The Writings of Nichiren Daishonin (Tokyo: Soka Gakkai, 1999), 131.

6. Ralph Waldo Emerson, "Man the Reformer," *Selected Works of Ralph Waldo Emerson,* vol. IV (from a lecture read before the Mechanics' Apprentices' Library Association, Boston, January 25, 1841).

7. Linus Pauling and Daisaku Ikeda, *A Lifelong Quest for Peace* (Sudbury, Ma.: Jones and Bartlett Publishers, 1992), cf-21.

8. Arnold Toynbee, *Civilization on Trial,* Oxford University Press, New York, 1948, 213.

9. Karl Jaspers, *Philosophy Is for Everyman,* trans. R.T.C. Hall and Wels (New York: Harcourt, Brace and World, Inc., 1967), 124.

Chapter Two: From a Century of War to a Century of Peace

1. Littleton, Colorado: On April 20, 1999, at Columbine High School in Littleton, two students went on a shooting rampage, injuring more than thirty people, some critically, and killing twelve before fatally shooting themselves.

2. Plato, *The Republic,* trans. Benjamin Jowett. Library of the Future, 4th ed. (Scr. 389: 646).

3. Plato, "Conversation with Callicles," *Gorgias,* trans. Benjamin Jowett (Grg. 482c).

4. Schlesinger, Arthur M., *A Thousand Days: John F. Kennedy in the White House* (Boston: Houghton Mifflin Company, 1965).

5. Alain: Pseudonym of Emile-Auguste Chartier (1868–1951).

Chapter Three: The Challenge To Bring Forth a New Reality

1. Steven R. Goldzwig, George N. Dionisopoulos and Halford R. Ryan, *In a Perilous Hour: The Public Address of John F. Kennedy* (Westport, Conn.: Greenwood Press, 1995), 182.

2. Julio Cortázar, *A Change of Light and Other Stories (Alguien que anda por ahi),* trans. Gregory Rabassa (New York: Knopf, 1980).

3. Quoted in Katherine Mayo, *Mother India* (New York: Harcourt Brace and Company, 1927), 393.

4. Johan Galtung and Daisaku Ikeda, *Choose Peace* (London: Pluto Press, 1995), 18.

Chapter Four: Peace Leadership

1. The main Web site of the Nuclear Age Peace Foundation is called Waging Peace (www.wagingpeace.org), with an auxiliary site called Nuclear Files (www.nuclearfiles.org). See p. 199 for more information.

Chapter Five: Children of the Nuclear Age

1. Cf. Mikhail Gorbachev and Daisaku Ikeda, *Niju-seiki no seishin no kyokun* (Moral lessons of the twentieth century) (Tokyo: Ushio Press, 1996).

2. Gulf of Tonkin incident: On August 2, 1964, the U.S. destroyer *Maddox* was collecting intelligence in the Gulf of Tonkin on the east coast of North Vietnam. North Vietnamese torpedo patrol boats attacked, and the U.S.S. *Ticonderoga* sent aircraft to repel the North Vietnamese, sinking one enemy vessel. Both the *Maddox* and another destroyer, the *C. Turner Joy*, were in the gulf again on August 4. When the captain of the *Maddox* claimed the ship was under attack, the two ships began firing into the night. The captain concluded hours later that there might not have been an actual attack. A reconnaissance jet pilot reported no trace of enemy vessels. President Lyndon Johnson lied about the attacks to the American people and ordered U.S. bombers to attack North Vietnam in "retaliation" for the attack that never happened. On August 7, Congress passed the Tonkin Gulf Resolution, allowing the president to "take all necessary measures to repel armed attack against the forces of the United States and to prevent further aggression," thus opening the door to the escalation of U.S. involvement in Vietnam.

Chapter Six: Conscientious Objection to War

1. Philip Yampolsky, ed., *Letters of Nichiren*, trans. Burton Watson (New York: Columbia University Press, 1996), 234.

2. Leo Tolstoy, *A Calendar of Wisdom: Daily Thoughts to Nourish the Soul*, trans. Peter Sekirin (London: Hodder & Stoughton, 1997).

3. Committee to Frame a World Constitution, *Preliminary Draft of a World Constitution* (Chicago: University of Chicago Press, 1948), 3.

Chapter Seven: Hiroshima and Nagasaki

1. Albert Camus, "Between Hell and Reason," *Combat,* August 8, 1945. (*Combat* was the French Resistance newspaper.)

2. Harry S. Truman, "Report to the Nation on the Potsdam Conference," August 9, 1945.

Chapter Eight: The Season of Hiroshima

1. David Krieger, "We Are All Culpable," see the Nuclear Age Peace Foundation Web site at www.wagingpeace.org.

2. General Lee Butler, "The Risks of Nuclear Deterrence: From Superpowers to Rogue Leaders," "National Press Club" (newsletter), February 2, 1998.

3. On August 14, 1996, the Canberra Commission on the Elimination of Nuclear Weapons presented its report to the Australian government and released it to the public.

4. Johan Galtung and Daisaku Ikeda, *Choose Peace* (London: Pluto Press, 1995), 142.

Chapter Nine: The Mission of Science

1. Dependent origination: A Buddhist doctrine expressing the interdependence of all things. It teaches that no being or phenomenon exists on its own but exists or occurs because of its relationship with other beings or phenomena. Everything in the world comes into existence in response to causes and conditions. In other words, nothing can exist independent of other things or arise in isolation.

2. The Consciousness-only (Skt Vijnanavada) school.

3. The Tiantai (Jpn Tendai) and Hua-yen (Jpn Kegon) schools.

Chapter Ten: The Challenge of Abolition 2000

1. According to the Carnegie Endowment for International Peace.

2. Comprehensive Test Ban Treaty: The 1963 Partial Test Ban Treaty (PTB) banned nuclear explosive tests in the atmosphere, under water and outer space. Testing was literally driven underground. The CTBT is designed to put an end to all explosive testing—although it does not

cover computer simulation and other laboratory testing techniques.

The treaty opened for signature in 1996 but will not take effect until 44 states designated by the accord as nuclear-capable have ratified it. Thirteen of those countries, including the United States, have yet to do so. The Senate rejected ratification of the treaty in October 1999, and the Bush administration has said it will not ask the Senate to reconsider its action.

3. Non-Proliferation Treaty Review Conference: Every five years, beginning in 1995, the signatory nations of the Nuclear Non-Proliferation Treaty meet to review the progress and implementation of the treaty's provisions. Designed to stop the spread of nuclear weapons, this treaty was originally signed in 1968 by the United States, the Soviet Union and Britain and since then by more than 180 nations. Signers declare themselves as nuclear weapons states or as non-nuclear weapons states. Non-nuclear weapons states promise not to acquire nuclear weapons and in return get help in developing nuclear power programs. Nuclear weapons states agree not to pass on nuclear weapons technology and also to cut back on and then begin negotiating a global ban on nuclear weapons.

4. The text of "Appeal to End the Nuclear Weapons Threat to Humanity and All Life" is available at the Nuclear Age Peace Foundation's Web site, www.wagingpeace.org. You can also add your signature to the appeal at this site.

5. Fissile Material Cutoff Treaty: A ban on the production of fissile material for nuclear weapons and other nuclear devices, considered an important objective for strengthening international security.

Chapter Eleven: The Abyss of Total Annihilation

1. Cf. Arnold Toynbee and Daisaku Ikeda, *Choose Life, A Dialogue* (New York: Oxford University Press, 1976), 315.

2. Quoted in Wayne Saslow, "Letters," "APS News," June 1999.

3. Josei Toda, *The Collected Works of Josei Toda*, vol. 3 (Tokyo: Seikyo Press, 1983), 32–33.

4. Josei Toda, *The Collected Works of Josei Toda*, vol. 4 (Tokyo: Seikyo Press, 1984), 565.

Chapter Twelve: Human Security and the Future of the United Nations

1. The Peace of Westphalia: This treaty, signed in Munster, Germany, on October 24, 1648, between the Holy Roman Emperor and the King of France, ended the Thirty Years War.

2. Projects in which the SGI has cooperated with the United Nations include the exhibitions "Nuclear Weapons, a Threat to Humanity" and "War and Peace," which have been shown in New York, Moscow, Beijing and Delhi.

Chapter Thirteen: Literature and Life

1. Shigeru Yoshido, *Kaiso junen* (Memoir, Ten Years) (Tokyo: Tokyo Shirakawa Shoin, 1982), 166.

2. Jean-Paul Sartre in *Le Monde*, April 1964.

Chapter 14: The Importance of Nongovernmental Organizations

1. The Worldwatch Institute, *The State of the World 2001* (Washington, D.C.: The Worldwatch Institute, 2001).

2. Quoted in *The New York Times*, December 4, 1997, A1.

3. John Milton, *The Complete Poems of John Milton*, ed. Charles W. Eliot (New York: P.F. Collier & Son, 1909), 360.

4. Blaise Pascal, *Pensées*, Section V (New York: Dutton, 1958), 298.

5. Tsunesaburo Makiguchi, *The Collected Works of Tsunesaburo Makiguchi*, vol. 6 ("The System of Value-Creating Pedagogy") (Tokyo: Daisan Bummeisha, 1983), 69.

Chapter Fifteen: The Role of Education

1. Pablo Neruda, *Cuándo de Chile* (Santiago, Chile: Austral, 1952).

Index

61–69; dialogue, a key to
peace, 65–66; family responses,
63–65; a woman of vision,
66–69
consciousness. *See* nine consciousnesses
consumerism, 101
corporate interests, influencing
democratic governments, 114,
164
Cortázar, Julio, 34–36
Costa Rica, 31
courage, 105–06; to remember,
73–74
Cousins, Norman, 72, 75
cowardice, of political leaders, 96
credibility, 45–46
crimes against humanity, violating
human security, 142
Cuban missile crisis, 127
Czech Republic, 35

D
Dante Alighieri, 145, 149
death, of death, 3; the destroyer
of worlds, 126
Decade for a Culture of Peace and
Non-Violence for the Children
of the World, 17, 117, 177
Declaration for the Abolition of
Nuclear Weapons, 25, 57, 131
democratic governments, corporate interests influencing, 114,
164
democratization, of dictatorships,
27
dependent origination, Buddhist
teachings on, 111
despair, struggling against, 122–23
deterrence, foolishness of, 142;
myth of, 52–54; theory of, 126
devil king, within minds of all
people, 130
dialogue, and action, 26–27; a key
to peace, 65–66

dictatorships, 35; democratization of, 27; fearing education,
39
dignity of life, the, Buddhist
teachings on, 124, 177
disparity, between rich and poor,
15
Dostoevsky, Fyodor, 145, 149–50
Drew, Wally, 69

E
Earth Summit, 161–62
education, dictatorships fearing,
39; encouraging the will to act,
175–77; hope for today's youth,
177–80; longtime associations
of the SGI-USA with, 30–31;
making us human, 30–31; role
of, 173–80; the SGI peace
movement, 174–75; in the
value of life, 57–58; the work
of, 168–69; for world citizenship, 144
Einstein, Albert, 7, 51, 72, 98, 106
Emerson, Ralph Waldo, 9
Eternal City, The, 151
ethical principles, 99–101
evil, absolute, 129–30. *See also*
good and evil

F
faith in youth, 131
Falk, Richard, 150
family responses, 63–65
Fate of the Earth, The, 3
Federal Republic of the World, 68
Fermi, Enrico, 59
Fissile Material Cutoff Treaty, 117
Fitzgerald, F. Scott, 150
folk tales, wisdom of, 103
foolishness, of deterrence, 142
Foundation, The. *See* Nuclear Age
Peace Foundation
Frankenstein, 102

Nagasaki no longer heard, 85–87. *See also* Hiroshima
Nanda, Ved, 119
Nanking Incident, 75
Napoleon, 31
nation-states, age of, 68
national security, dependent upon global security, 143–44
national sovereignty, supporters of, 143
Native American peoples, genocide against, 88
NATO nations, 121
Nazism, Camus' struggle against, 72; German people under, 81
need to abolish war, 137–38
need to win peace each day, 43
Neruda, Pablo, 150, 155, 157, 179
networks, global news, 14
New Agenda Coalition, 82, 116
new reality, a, education making us human, 30–31; good and evil as two aspects of the human mind, 33–34; human revolution, the path to a hopeful future, 34–36; power of education, 38–40; revival of the imagination, 31–33; sowing seeds of peace, 36–37; unflagging optimism, 37–38
New York Times, The, 115
New Yorker, The, 80–81
news networks, global, 14
Newseum, 51
Nichiren, 8, 64, 108
nine consciousnesses, Buddhist teaching of, 106–07
Nixon, Richard, 61
Nobel Peace Prize, 9, 53, 165
Non-Proliferation Treaty (NPT), present regimes of the, 81, 116–17
Non-Proliferation Treaty Review and Extension Conference, 113
nongovernmental organizations

(NGOs), 161–71; accepting goal of abolition, 123; building transnational solidarity among, 47–48, 118; holding the key, 114; imperative of uniting, 169–71; and the power of an individual, 167–68; power of commitment and compassion, 165–66; renaming, 166; representing interests of ordinary people, 163–65; and the sovereignty of conscience, 166–67; supporting the New Agenda Coalition, 116; the work of education, 168–69
nuclear abolition movement, 4, 76, 79–80
nuclear accidents, 126
Nuclear Age, children of the, 59; a critical break with the past, 52; dangers of the, 7, 45; escaping the, 127; ethical ruin of the, 5; initiation of the, 125; making time more precious, 143; transcending the, 91–131
Nuclear Age Peace Foundation (NAPF), 18, 22, 45–46, 52, 115; building, 45–47; founders of the, 69; on the Internet, 47; "Sowing Seeds of Peace," 36–37; Youth Advisory Council, 178; Youth Outreach Coordinator, 178
nuclear-armed states, 14–15, 84, 119
"Nuclear Arms, Threat to Our World," 85
Nuclear Non-Proliferation Treaty. *See* Non-Proliferation Treaty
nuclear power plants, 94
nuclear priesthood, faded homilies of the, 83
"nuclear puzzle," 84
nuclear weapons, 74, 94–96

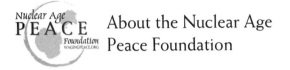

About the Nuclear Age Peace Foundation

The Nuclear Age Peace Foundation's vision is a world at peace, free of the threat of war and free of weapons of mass destruction. The Foundation's mission is to advance initiatives to eliminate the threat of nuclear weapons to all life, to foster the global rule of law, and to build an enduring legacy of peace through education and advocacy.

Founded in 1982, the Nuclear Age Peace Foundation (NAPF) is a non-profit, non-partisan, international education and advocacy organization. In 2002, the Foundation celebrates twenty years of service to the local, national and international communities.

NAPF initiates and supports worldwide efforts to abolish nuclear weapons, to strengthen international law and institutions, to use technology responsibly and sustainably, and to empower young people to create a more peaceful world.

For more information on NAPF, its programs and how to get involved, visit the Foundation's principle Web site:

Nuclear Age
Peace Foundation   www.wagingpeace.org

We also encourage you to visit the following Web sites:

The Nuclear Files   www.nuclearfiles.org

Abolition 2000   www.abolition2000.org

Moving Beyond
Missile Defense   www.mbmd.org

End of Existence   www.endofexistence.org

About the Soka Gakkai
International

The Soka Gakkai International (SGI) is an ethnically diverse Buddhist association with more than 12 million members in more than 180 countries. SGI members embrace the philosophy of Nichiren, a 13th-century Buddhist teacher and reformer. Inspired by his life-affirming teachings, SGI's ultimate aim is the realization of a peaceful world.

For SGI members, Buddhism is a practical philosophy of individual empowerment and inner transformation that enable people to develop themselves, overcome life's inevitable challenges, and positively influence their community, society and the world.

Activities that promote peace, culture and education are central to the SGI and range from discussion circles on local concerns to conferences and exhibitions on global concerns. Such activities typically seek to raise people's awareness of the themes of peace, environmental protection and human rights.

For more information on the SGI, its activities and how to get involved, visit any of the following Web sites:

Soka Gakkai International	www.sgi.org
Soka Gakkai International-USA	www.sgi-usa.org
Victory Over Violence	www.vov.com
Toda Institute for Global Peace	www.toda.org
Boston Research Center for the 21st Century	www.brc21.org

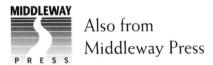

Also from Middleway Press

For the Sake of Peace: Seven Paths to Global Harmony,
A Buddhist Perspective, by Daisaku Ikeda
Winner of the NAPRA Nautilus Award 2002 for Social Change
(Paperback: ISBN 0-9674697-9-1; $14.00.
Hardcover: ISBN 0-9674697-2-4; $25.95)

"At a time when we squander enormous amounts of human
and environmental resources on the study of and preparation
for making war, *For the Sake of Peace* stands as a primary text in
the study and practice of making peace."

—NAPRA, Nautilus Award citation

"...a passionate, intelligent plea for mindfulness in both individual and societal action."

—*ForeWord* magazine

Soka Education: A Buddhist Vision for Teachers, Students and Parents,
by Daisaku Ikeda
(ISBN 0-9674697-4-0; $23.95)

From the Japanese word meaning "to create value," this book
presents a fresh spiritual perspective to question the ultimate
purpose of education. Mixing American pragmatism with Buddhist philosophy, the goal of Soka education is the lifelong
happiness of the learner.

"[Teachers] will be attracted to Soka and Ikeda's plea that educators bring heart and soul back to education."

—*Teacher* magazine

"Ikeda's practical perscription places students' needs first, empowers teachers, and serves as a framework for global citizenship."

—George David Miller, professor, Lewis University

The Way of Youth: Buddhist Common Sense for Handling Life's Questions, by Daisaku Ikeda
(ISBN 0-9674697-0-8; $14.95)

"[This book] shows the reader how to flourish as a young person in the world today; how to build confidence and character in modern society; learn to live with respect for oneself and others; how to contribute to a positive, free and peaceful society; and find true personal happiness."

—Midwest Book Review

The Buddha in Your Mirror:
Practical Buddhism and the Search for Self,
by Woody Hochswender, Greg Martin and Ted Morino
(Paperback: ISBN0-9674697-8-3; $14.00
Hardcover: ISBN 0-9674697-1-6; $23.95)

A bestselling Buddhist primer that reveals the most modern, effective and practical way to achieve what is called enlightenment or Buddhahood. Based on the centuries-old teaching of the Japanese Buddhist master Nichiren, this method has been called the "direct path" to enlightenment.

"Like the Buddha, this book offers practical guidelines to overcome difficulties in everyday life and to be helpful to others. Readers will find these pages are like a helpful and supportive friend. I enthusiastically recommend it."

—Dr. David Chappell, editor of
Buddhist Peacework: Creating Cultures of Peace